#2 Sister Lena Beideck in a portrait from 1941, as she neared retirement

#3 Sister Wilma Loehrig in front of Tabor Home in the early 1940s, when her reign as head deaconess was just beginning

'TWAS A HARD KNOCK LIFE

The Tabor Home Story

Editor:

Orville Wright Jr.

ISBN 0-7414-3775-9

Published by:

INFINITY
PUBLISHING.COM

1094 New DeHaven Street, Suite 100
West Conshohocken, PA 19428-2713
Info@buybooksontheweb.com
www.buybooksontheweb.com
Toll-free (877) BUY BOOK
Local Phone (610) 941-9999
Fax (610) 941-9959

Printed in the United States of America

Printed on Recycled Paper

Published February 2007

FOREWORD

Some of the Tabor Home alumni, especially those who had been residents of Tabor Home during the '30s, '40s and '50s, established a lovely tradition of gathering socially once or twice a year. When I came to work at Tabor in 1989 I began to attend their annual pool parties and luncheons. The warmth of family pervaded these gatherings, which were filled with recollections of their earlier life at Tabor Home.

Fred Plequette, an alumnus who was active on the Tabor Services board of trustees, would often speak about his years at Tabor Home. Later, after he resigned from the board in early 2001, Fred sent me a tape he recorded of his Tabor Home memories. A number of our trustees expressed how important it would be to secure the recollections of other Tabor alumni.

The missing talent for this memories project appeared in person when Orville Wright Jr., a Tabor alumnus with an extraordinary range of skills, visited Tabor in early 2003. A recent retiree, Orv had served as Commander in the U.S. Navy and as Aerospace Manager for IBM and Lockheed Martin. Orv initially approached me with one volunteer idea: to encourage youth now in the care of Tabor Children's Services to gain skills to succeed in life. This offer led to Orv's job interview workshops in the agency's current life skills programs, where he has been an inspiration to our at-risk youth. From the first meeting with Orv it was clear that he felt an abiding connection to Tabor Home and its former residents. He also had been polishing his own written memories. Not only did he respond enthusiastically when asked to help bring Tabor's memories project to fruition, Orv also conceived the strategy for eliciting stories from alumni who might not be writers. Since March 2006 Orv has served as trustee on the Tabor Services board.

He and I presented the idea at the Tabor Alumni luncheon in October 2003. During the next two years Orv followed every lead to reach additional alumni. In April 2005 a feature story in a major Bucks County daily, the Intelligencer, highlighted the memories project.

This book is offered as part of Tabor's 2007-2008 celebration of 100 years of giving direction to children and youth in need. Inspired by the men and women who grew up at Tabor Home where they learned values that prepared them for life, and grateful to the Tabor alumni who shared their memories, the board and staff of Tabor Children's Services remain dedicated to the agency's important mission of keeping children safe, strengthening families and promoting independence.

Ariana Burrows
Chief Development Officer
Tabor Children's Services

INTRODUCTION

When the idea of publishing the memories of Tabor Home alumni was proposed, my first reaction was that it would be the ideal format to convey to readers what it was like growing up in a children's home. It became evident early on that the vast majority of potential authors lacked the confidence to put pen to paper and submit their recollections. A scheme was established to interview any interested participant and draft their remembrances for their review. This approach proved to be a workable strategy.

This anthology is divided into chapters by decades, starting with the 1920s and concluding with the 1980s. Sadly, several of the older authors died before seeing their stories published.

The genesis of Tabor Home for Children occurred in 1907. Mrs. Emma Chidester of the Tabor Evangelical Lutheran Church in Philadelphia offered her suburban residence in Cheltenham, a nearby town in the adjacent county, as a home for destitute children. The congregation of the Tabor Church elected a board of trustees, and the state courts chartered the Home.

A serious problem arose when the Cheltenham School Board refused to admit Philadelphia children. The school-aged children were transferred to the former residence of the Reverend Philip Lamartine, at 111 Wyoming Avenue in Philadelphia, from which they could attend public school. The younger children stayed at Mrs. Chidester's home. The cost of maintaining two homes proved too expensive, so a year later a single residence on East Tabor Road in Olney was rented.

A real breakthrough occurred in 1913, when Tabor Home acquired the Fretz estate, a magnificent property located in Doylestown, Pa., 30 miles north of Philadelphia. Situated on nearly 100 acres of rich farmland, the estate contained a mansion, carriage house and laundry building, and also included a large barn and quarters for a tenant farmer.

Following this move, the church and the board of Tabor

Home arranged for a change of charter, by which the Home became autonomous. Although staffed with Deaconesses from the Philadelphia motherhouse, the church no longer elected the Tabor Home board. Financial support came partly from local and state government, and the courts determined which children entered the Home and their length of stay. A small number of orphans were assigned to Tabor by the courts, but most of the children in residence came from broken homes and had at least one parent living. Without the daycare options now available, single parents who did not live near extended family had difficulty providing care for their children during the workday. Some parents sent contributions towards the care of their children.

In reality, the head administrator at Tabor Home established the rules of conduct and decided whether a child should remain, based upon behavior. The two head administrators who managed the Home for five decades, Sister Lena Beideck and Sister Wilma Loehrig, dominate stories of the first 70 years of Tabor Home. Their names appear repeatedly in the memories of the children who grew up at this venerable institution.

A confluence of events contributed to the eventual demise of Tabor Home as a residential institution for needy children. In the 1970s, the number of children assigned to the Home started to decrease dramatically. For instance, from a full house of 80 children a year in the 1960s, 50 were being cared for in 1970. That number dropped to 34 only two years later. In addition, the reasons children came to the Home changed by the 1970s. Instead of single parents requesting that Tabor Home care for their children, the courts sent children who had been removed from their parents because of abuse or neglect and youth who had involvement with the juvenile justice system. A third factor was the growing belief among child-development professionals that institutions did not prepare children for adult family life as well as foster care would. The expense of maintaining places like Tabor Home was also substantial.

In the early 1970s the board of directors decided to change the tone of Tabor from a Lutheran, religious-based Home to a non-sectarian, private nonprofit organization. The change became official in 1978, and a year later the name was changed to Tabor Children's Services Inc.

The written memories of the authors underwent an editing process to enhance readability, but no attempt was made to purge unpleasant or unsightly remembrances. Facts have a way of changing in an individual's long-term memory. Therefore, some inconsistency may be noticed when the same story is told by several people.

This centennial project is dedicated to the thousands of children who experienced adolescence at Tabor Home and had their lives profoundly influenced by the encounter. I am confident that every reader will be affected by the events recorded so honestly by the individual authors.

Orville Wright Jr.
Tabor Home 1941-1951

TABLE OF CONTENTS

Chapter One - The 1920s

MEMORIES FROM THE FARMER'S DAUGHTER
By Betty Berger Porter

One of my earliest memories of Tabor Home was being with my mother in the farmhouse during a thunderstorm. Dad was in the process of getting all the cows into their stalls when I observed a bolt of lightning enter the open door of the barn. Dad later relayed the details of how it knocked all the cows down to their knees and exited the far door that Harry Burmeister had opened to check on the remainder of the herd. Harry also fell in a prone position, more surprised than injured, as the bolt departed. In addition to the trauma associated with nature's power, the cows refused to give a single drop of milk that evening.

For most of the time that I was at Tabor Home, we kept two teams of horses (four in all) for plowing the fields and lifting hay into the mow after it was harvested. I recall my father brought a new horse from the Pocono Mountains and shortly thereafter hitched it to an open wagon and took me with him into Doylestown. In the middle of town a trolley came along and spooked the horse. In an attempt to calm the animal, Dad jumped off the wagon and ran forward, turning the reins over to me. I was just 8 or 9 years old and had never really driven a horse and wagon on my own. He finally got the horse calmed down, but I wasn't sure what I would have done had the horse sprinted away with me trying to control him. It was quite an ordeal and made a lasting impression on me.

Bringing in the hay was always a memorable event, because it required teamwork and coordination. After the hay was cut, it was raked into long rows by a mechanical rake and then manually forked into mounds. The hay wagon would come along and the hay would be lifted into the wagon with long pitchforks. When the fully loaded wagon reached the barn, a U-shaped fork attached to a rope and pulley would be inserted into the pile. A finger-like device would then hold the hay until a trip lanyard was pulled, dropping the load into the mow.

On several occasions I saw the boys play a practical joke by putting a new kid on the wagon to put the fork into the hay. A horse would be used to elevate the hay from the wagon to the mow. The pranksters would order the horse to start pulling before the greenhorn could get off the pile. They all had a good laugh as the novice tumbled backwards off the ascending mound of hay.

Mrs. Porter was the daughter of Henry (Harry J.) Berger, who was the farmer at Tabor Home from 1922 until 1940. Betty was 4 years old when her father initially accepted employment at the Home. She lived in the farmhouse at Tabor until she graduated from college in 1939. She currently resides in Newtown, Pa.

TABOR IN THE 1920s - THE GOOD OLD DAYS
By Fred Plequette

My brother Otto and I, accompanied by a caseworker, took the trolley from Philadelphia to Tabor Home on a spring day in 1922. It was the first time we had ever been out of the city, and I was mesmerized by the fields of wheat that appeared to be moving like a vast expanse of ocean. Of course, at the time I did not even know what wheat was or that it grew in large fields in the ground. Little did I realize how much I was about to learn about farming in the next 10 years.

Sister Lena Beideck met us in the big house and took us over to the boys' dormitory. I was initially struck by the 29 beds in the open bay on the second floor. All were neatly made up with white counterpane. The first order of business was to get a number assigned so all of our clothes could be identified. Mine was 35 and Otto's was 33. One's number was seared into your brain, and, even after 70 years, 35 sounds as familiar as my name.

In 1913, Tabor Home had acquired a one-hundred-acre farm from the estate of the Fretz family, a well-to-do Doylestown family. It consisted of a three-story mansion, a laundry building and a large structure that housed the carriages and horses. The carriage house was renovated to become the boys' dorm, and the mansion was used as both the girls' dormitory and staff offices. The dining room was located on the main floor of the big house and could seat all 80 children at once.

Daily Routine

All children had chores both indoors and on the farm or grounds. Of course, everyone made his own bed. I scrubbed the dining room floors once a week and later was assigned responsibility for the chicken house, which required cleaning periodically and involved transporting clean straw from the barn. In addition, I fed the chickens and collected the eggs. Ensuring the coal-burning water heater had enough coal was another chore I was assigned. In the summer, everyone pitched in to weed the truck patch, pick up potatoes, bring in the hay and harvest the corn. We didn't use much machinery on the farm because of the expense, and child labor was readily available.

The girls were expected to tend to all the chores in the kitchen, including preparing the food, and washing and drying the dishes. They would also skim the cream off the unpasteurized milk and crank the churn to produce butter. Because of the small amount generated, only the staff members were served butter. The kids ate margarine.

Sports

Sports played a big part in the lives of Tabor boys. We were always playing baseball or football whenever we had any free time. The field between the girls' and boys' houses was the most common place to play, although we occasionally used the meadow where the cows roamed. Avoiding cow plops was all-important. We also played a game called peggy. It utilized a seven-inch piece of broom handle (the peg) sharpened on both ends and a three- or four-foot broom handle that was used as the bat. The batter would strike the peg, which jumped into the air and allow the batter to hit it. The fielders would attempt to catch the peg and throw it into a rectangular box at "home plate." If they were successful, they would assume the role of batter. I am not sure if we made this game up at Tabor, but I have never heard of it outside of the Home.

Everyone played marbles. A 10- or 12-foot diameter circle would be drawn with a stick in the smooth dirt, and the marbles would be dumped into the circle. From outside the circle, each participant would attempt to knock as many marbles as possible out of the circle with their "shooter." We would either play for fun (no exchange of marbles) or for keeps. Losing your favorite marbles could be traumatic, and tears would occasionally accompany a younger child's loss.

Fishing in the local bodies of water was a common pastime. Before an in-ground pool was constructed next to the boys' house, we would swim in the Neshaminy Creek or the smaller creek that ran behind the barn. Someone had tied a rope to an over-hanging limb, and it was great fun to swing into the water. After the pool was built, we did most of our swimming there. No chemicals were used to treat the algae, so in short order a green slime would accumulate on the side of the pool. Several times a season the pool would be drained, scrubbed clean and refilled with fresh water; and then the process would start all over again.

Activities

Berry picking was big in the summertime. Cherry trees were plentiful on the grounds, and we often climbed the trees, and broke off limbs of cherries and later recovered them. We also picked strawberries, mulberries and blackberries, all growing wild in the woods. We would walk over to the National Farm School, located about three miles away. They had apple orchards and didn't mind if we scooped up a handful of ripe apples that had fallen off the trees.

Some of our games were not gentle. We would put an orange in the foot of our knee socks and use it like a weapon, hitting other kids. We were careful never to use a rock, for obvious reasons.

May Day was very big at Tabor. It was an open house, and about a thousand people would visit for a meal and a religious service, and to make purchases from vendors selling various items in booths set up on the grounds. Alumni of the Home would often use this event to return and visit Tabor. The meal would consist of homemade potato salad, ham, vegetables, coffee and dessert.

There were very few ways to earn money at Tabor. Some of the boys would walk up to the Doylestown Country Club and caddy on the weekends. The going price for 18 holes was a dollar. A side benefit was finding lost golf balls and making homemade clubs to hit the balls into the meadow.

A favorite activity of all the children was sledding and ice-skating. We would play ice hockey on the natural ice that formed in the area between the buildings or go down to Beanies' dam, which was located across the road not too far from the barn. The long curving driveways made sledding a real adventure as long as you didn't lose control and end up on the highway. We all loved winter!

Holidays

Four holidays stand out as memorable when I reflect on my days at Tabor. Halloween was fun, as the ground and first floors were decorated. Thanksgiving was the time that alumni from the Home would return and join us for a turkey dinner. We were always glad to see all the "big guys" return and share stories of the outside world with us. Sometimes they would take us hunting for rabbits and serve that as well.

We all looked forward to Easter, because it meant a basket of goodies for each child. In addition, a local candy store would create the largest Easter egg we ever saw. It must have weighed 10 or 15 pounds and was made of chocolate and pure sugar. They would donate the egg to the Home, and each kid would get to share in the demise of the giant confection.

Christmas, however, was everyone's favorite holiday. There were large decorated trees in each house plus a religious manger scene. Service clubs would donate gifts, and each child would get several small gifts (usually clothing) to carry back to his or her cubicle. Everyone would go to church, and a joyful spirit permeated the entire Home at Christmas.

Education

The small cottage located about 100 yards south of the boys' house was used as a one-room school when I arrived at Tabor in 1922. Mrs. Archer was the teacher, and she worked for the school district. The following year, all the kids walked to the Edison School, which had two rooms: first through fourth grades in one room and fifth through eighth in the second room. After graduating from the eighth grade, we all went to Doylestown High School, located one mile north of Tabor.

Concluding Thoughts

As I reminisce about the 10 years I lived at Tabor, I feel I was quite lucky to be raised by generous and caring Sisters who took good care of all the children. Over the years, when former Tabor kids reunited, they often reminisced about the good old days in the 1930s.

After graduating from Doylestown High, I got a job in Philadelphia that lasted almost two years and paid the princely sum of $1.00 for a nine-hour day. It was depression time and jobs were hard to come by, and as I look back, those were not the "good old days."

On May 22, 1922, Fred and his brother Otto came to Tabor at age 8 and 6, respectively, and Fred remained there until graduating from Doylestown High School 10 years later. From 1965 to 2001 Fred E. Plequette served on the Tabor Services board of trustees. He died in June 2003 at the age of 89.

7

THIS WAS OUR HOME
By Ida Stafford Fenstermacher

The Staffords may have been the largest family to live together in the history of Tabor Home. In addition to George, my twin brother, there were Helen, Bill and Sarah, who was only 2 years old when we came to Tabor. I really don't remember my mother, who died just before we were put in the Home. I recall living with my godmother for one year prior to Tabor. We lived in Doylestown, so it was just a short trip down Route 611.

Sister Lena Beideck was the head matron in charge, and all the kids adored her. I felt very special because my birthday and Sister Lena's were on the same day, February 24th, and she always included me during the celebration and fanfare of her birthday.

Looking back at life at Tabor in the 1920s and 1930s, I have nothing but fond memories. May Day was always a great deal of fun when the kids would get dressed up and put on skits. We would sing and dance and have a grand time. Halloween was another holiday that the children would create or borrow homemade costumes and parade around in a make-believe world in which we all participated. Of course, Christmas was special and we all looked forward to getting gifts.

The boys and girls lived in separate buildings, and the girls were housed six or eight to a room. No one felt deprived or put upon. This was our home. Our father was working in Philadelphia at that time, so we saw him quite often.

Several memories stand out as I view life 80 years ago. I distinctly recall walking to Doylestown to St. Paul's Lutheran Church to prepare for church membership. I was the only Tabor girl in my confirmation class, but Fred Strowig, Bob Ralston and John Clark were boys in my class. There were several swimming holes across Easton Road and behind the barn where we spent many an afternoon enjoying life in the summer.

When I was a junior in high school I obtained a job in a hosiery mill in Philadelphia, and that ended my formal education. My brother George worked for the same company. Several years later in 1935, I married Edwin Fenstermacher, and my life headed in a completely different direction.

Ida Stafford Fenstermacher and her twin brother George came to Tabor in 1922 at the age of 5 years. Ida lived in Willow Grove, Pa., until her death at age 88 in July 2004.

FROM OUTSIDE THE TENT
By Kathryn McDowell Stafford

My memories of Tabor Home are quite different from all the rest in this book, as I never spent a day in the Home. From the title you can see that all my remembrances are second-hand through my husband, George Stafford.

George was one of five Staffords who came to Tabor Home in 1921. He was age 4, and remained there until 1933. He and his sister Ida were twins, and they felt they had a special relationship with the head matron, Sister Lena Beideck, because their birthdays fell on the same day. At Tabor, a Lutheran-affiliated organization, evening devotions and prayers played a large role in the upbringing and values of the children. Each child was permitted to choose his or her favorite hymn on their birthday, which made them feel quite important. For George and Ida, it was a really big deal to share their birthday with Sister Lena, the woman most of the children associated with their own mother.

I met George in Willow Grove Park several years after he left Tabor Home. We got married four years later and for the next 50 plus years, I never heard him say anything negative about Tabor Home. He spoke very highly of the Home and on more than one occasion would comment, "Thank God for Tabor Home."

I must confess when I found out George was raised in a home, I felt sorry for him, but I later concluded that he actually had it better than I did growing up. After he left Tabor in the 1930s, he would thumb his way up to Doylestown from Willow Grove, Pa., and help Harry J. Berger and Boog Burmeister with the farming chores.

The cottage at the end of the back lane at Tabor was a school for the children during grades one through three. One day George was the last child into the room, and he left the school door wide-open. Sister Sophie, who taught all three grades, suggested George go back and close the door. George reacted by running out the door and across the field. Sister Sophie was up to the challenge. She sprinted after him and boxed his ears as she led him back to class and supervised his closing the door. George probably learned a valuable lifetime lesson with regard to running away from problems! He also found out that a deaconess' uniform was no barrier while running.

George was sworn in as a policeman on the day after the Japanese attacked Pearl Harbor. He enlisted in the U.S. Navy in 1943 as a ship fitter, and operated in the Atlantic theater during the war. I still remember the day he returned home, December 13, 1945, a glorious day.

After completing 25 years in the police force, he retired and joined Bell Telephone for a second career. Dr. Walter McKinney, a Tabor Home board member, played a big part in assisting George both at the Home and after he left and lived in Philadelphia. He always had the highest admiration for the doctor.

Sadly, George passed away in 1993, but I am convinced that he felt being raised at Tabor Home assisted him in coping with all the challenges that life brought his way.

.

Kathryn McDowell Stafford was not a Tabor Home alumna, but she was married to George Stafford for more than 50 years. She lives in Warminster, Pa.

WE HAD FAR FEWER OPTIONS IN THE OLD DAYS
By Harry Clark

I came to Tabor from Philadelphia with my older brother John. The one memory that stuck in my mind all these years was sleeping in the same bed with my brother the very first night.

My years at Tabor Home were really quite enjoyable. It was great fun having so many kids to play with. We all loved football, baseball and basketball. We would get up a game at the drop of a hat. Tabor kids were excellent athletes and made quite a name for themselves at Doylestown High School in the 1930s.

The one incident I regret involved staying out for dinner and getting into a misunderstanding with Sister Martha, who was temporarily in charge when Sister Lena was recovering from a minor illness. The discussion got heated and resulted in my being asked to leave. Dr. McKinney drove me to my grandmother's house in Philly but she was unable to care for me, so I finally went to live with an aunt in Ardsley. The only other regret I had about the Home was beyond my control. That was that our mother never came by to see us in all the years John and I were at Tabor.

My first job in the real world was as a soda jerk in Norristown. I got the job by answering an ad in the local newspaper. I forget how much the job paid, but it wasn't enough to live on. When I was old enough I joined the Merchant Marine with the thought of seeing the world and being paid for it. After four and one half years of sea duty I was scheduled to leave New York harbor for an Atlantic run just after the start of World War II. My girl friend (later my wife) gave me an ultimatum that if I got on that ship, I could kiss her goodbye forever. As they say, love conquers all, and I chose not to show up when the ship set sail. A week later a German U-boat sank my ship, and all hands on board perished at sea. My decision to go AWOL (absent without leave) remains the best choice I have ever made in my life.

I was drafted into the Army and served three and one half years until the war ended. If I had my live to live over again, I would choose to spend my childhood at Tabor Home. That's how much I appreciated the Home!

Harry was 5 years old in 1923 when he initially came to Tabor Home. He left 13 years later involuntarily and was essentially on his own until he joined the Merchant Marine prior to World War II. Harry presently resides in Upper Darby, Pa.

IF YOU THINK THINGS ARE TOUGH TODAY ...
By Fred Strowig

My sister Ernestine, age 4, and I were living in Philadelphia just prior to checking in to Tabor in the middle of winter with a foot of snow on the ground. My earliest recollection of that day was seeing Anna Ralston with her head shaved bald. Apparently, she had contracted lice and that was the accepted procedure.

I came with a huge disadvantage. I could only speak German. Trying to learn anything in school without understanding the language was impossible. I failed the first grade and spent the summer learning the English language. All Tabor kids in the first three grades went to school at the Cottage School, which was under the auspices of the Doylestown Township School. Mrs. Archer was the teacher.

One of my early memories is how hard it was to earn spending money. At 10 years of age, a few of us (Otto Plequette, Herb Wohlfarth and Phil Pfaft) would occasionally caddy at the Doylestown Country Club. For 18 holes we would be paid $0.75, and be thankful for that amount.

Athletics always played a big part in the lives of Tabor boys in the 1930s. We really made an impact in the BuxMont league in all sports. Al Sulak started for the varsity basketball team; Johnny Clark was shortstop for the baseball team; Herb Wohlfarth played end in football; Phil Pfaft was selected All-BuxMont center on the football team (his brother Frank played guard); and Bob Ralston was captain of both the football and basketball teams. In all modesty, I was co-captain of the baseball team and quite an accomplished pitcher. It was no wonder that the athletic director, Bill Wolfe, stated, "What Doylestown needs are more Tabor Home kids on our teams. They are fearless."

When I graduated from high school, the country was in the middle of a depression and jobs were really scarce. I worked at Nyce's Shoe Store for a year before Dr. McKinney used his influence and got me a job with the Pennsylvania Liquor Control Board in Philadelphia as a file clerk at a salary of $75.00 a month. It sure beat caddying for $0.75 a round.

Fred came to Tabor Home in 1925 at the age of 7. He remained there until the summer of 1937, one year after graduating from Doylestown High School. Fred presently lives in Havertown, Pa.

THE LONGEVITY RECORD AT TABOR IS MINE
By Ernestine Strowig Pilant

The first day at Tabor Home was quite frightening as you can imagine it would be for any child who has not yet reached her fourth birthday. It was doubly so because my brother Fred and I could only speak German when we were delivered to the Home by social workers. They took my brother away (to the boys' house as it turned out) and showed me to a room in the girls' house. It was one of the worst days of my life.

The whole first year was quite a nightmare as I entered kindergarten and attempted to learn ABCs and numbers in a language I did not comprehend. Freddy had similar problems in the first grade. Eventually, it all worked out, because kids can learn language skills quite rapidly and adjust to changing conditions much easier than adults.

The best part of living at Tabor was my association with the other children, as well as living in beautiful Bucks County. It was actually a lot of fun learning life skills such as canning fruits and vegetables, ironing clothes and doing the laundry. The good work ethic that was established early in life at Tabor paid great dividends in my adult life. It was especially enjoyable associating with the boys as they took turns in the kitchen drying dishes. We were often not a model household as we stung each other with damp dishtowels. A direct hit on the leg would really smart, but there was always retaliation!

Another aspect of the daily routine that I liked as I got older was taking care of the younger children by reading bedtime stories, helping them with their prayers and supervising brushing of teeth. Perhaps part of my pleasure was knowing how welcome the support from older girls was when I was young.

One of the down sides of living at Tabor was personal and didn't have anything to do with the rules or regulations with which we had to abide. It was the terrible realization that our parents were not concerned enough with us to take the trouble to visit us on a routine basis. Were it not for my aunt and uncle on my father's side, we would have had no contact with relatives during our tenure at the Home. It was very disturbing for a young child to face that type of rejection.

My last few years in high school I spent weekends working as a housekeeper for a local family. After graduating, I continued working full-time for 12 months with the same family to save money for nursing training at Chestnut Hill Hospital.

I corresponded with Sister Lena for a number of years after leaving the Home, and her letters are among some of my most cherished possessions. She was the closest thing I had to a mother growing up.

Although it is a difficult life for a young girl, I think the years at Tabor Home prepared me for a successful career in nursing, as well as the U.S. Army and married life. I look back with mixed feelings, but they are mostly positive.

Ernestine and her brother Fred came to Tabor Home in January 1925. She was almost 4 years old and would remain at Tabor one year after she graduated from Doylestown High School. She entered nursing training and eventually joined the Nurse Corps in the U.S. Army just several months before the ending of hostilities in 1945. Ernestine resides in Williamsburg, Va.

HALLOWEEN WAS MY FAVORITE TIME
By Kathy Berger Coulton

My family, the Bergers, consisting of three girls and two boys, was living in Coaldale, Pa., when my parents divorced in the mid-1920s. I am not sure if incompatible religions were the root cause, but dad was Lutheran and mother was Catholic. My father worked in the coal mines and on the railroad. He heard about Tabor Home through the Lutheran Church and attempted to enroll the whole family. The boys' dormitory was completely full, so only my older sister Myrtle, younger sister Helen and I were admitted.

The first day at the Home was fairly traumatic for Helen (3 years old), but when I spotted all the available toys, I thought to myself, "What a great place." Helen just sat in the corner and cried.

As I reminisce about life as it was 75 years ago, I realize I always liked it at Tabor. Sister Lena was like a mother to me, and I think a lot of the children felt that way also. The girls, by and large, stayed out of trouble. It was always the boys that ended up standing on the stage during meal hours or being punished for doing something stupid and getting caught.

I don't want to leave the impression that I was a "goodie two shoes." I remember one night in the summer that five of us crept down the fire escape with our swimsuits on and jumped over the locked gate and into the swimming pool, which was located adjacent to the boys' house. We were very careful to remain quiet and not splash to attract any attention. Suddenly, Sister Jenny and Sister Helma, in bathing suits, unlocked the gate and commenced swimming in the shallow end. I'm not sure either of them knew how to swim. We all cowered at the deep end in the shadows which gave us some protection against being detected. After 15 or 20 minutes they dried off, locked the gate and were gone. Talk about dodging a bullet; we all felt so lucky! We immediately called it an evening and congratulated ourselves on being so clever to beat the system. Alas, it was not actually our lucky night. Jeff, Sister Lena's dog, heard us as we ascended the fire escape to return to our rooms and alerted his mistress. We had no sooner returned to our beds in total darkness than the flipping light switch illuminated our room, and there stood Sister Lena, not smiling. It would have been hard to explain how five girls with wet bathing suits and damp hair had been in bed all night. Nor did we even have an opportunity to explain. "I will see you all in my office tomorrow," intoned Sister Lena as she turned off the lights and abruptly departed. None of us slept too soundly that evening.

After expressing "keen disappointment" in our behavior, she rendered the verdict, which was not open to appeal. We were banned from swimming for two weeks and given extra chores in the kitchen, which may not seem like too harsh a sentence, but the next two weeks were the hottest of the summer. I think most of us learned our lesson.

Although Christmas and May Day were both fun holidays, my favorite was always Halloween. I think it was because it was a time to demonstrate one's creativity. After dinner all the kids would dress up in costumes that were stored in boxes in the attic, and then everyone would gather in the boys' dormitory. As the music played, the disguised children would parade past Sister Lena as she attempted to identify the incognito participants. There would be great peals of laughter as she failed in her attempts. Following the parade, tubs of water were scattered about for us to bob for apples, and bags of candy and other goodies were distributed. What fun that was!

In 1938 Sister Lena took ill and was granted a temporary leave of absence as head matron. Sister Marie Burgstrom, who was very strict and a no-nonsense type of supervisor, replaced her temporarily. It seemed to me that the children who were there as wards of the state (i.e. their parents paid nothing to the Home for their support) were targeted for expulsion. I was pulled out of the tenth grade and sent to take care of a 3-year-old child for a couple in Narberth, Pa. The parents weren't very nice to me and treated me like an indentured servant. After a year, I quit and obtained a similar job in Jenkintown for a very nice couple. The husband was the artist who painted a portrait of Sister Lena. That employment lasted three years. In 1942, I got married and got on with my real life.

Kathy Berger was 5 years old in 1927 when she came to Tabor Home with her sisters, Myrtle and Helen. The Jenkintown artist who painted Sister Lena, Ralph Coleman, gifted the painting to Tabor Home in Kathy's honor. Kathy Berger presently resides in North Wales, Pa.

Chapter Two - The 1930s

I PITCHED FOR THE TABOR BASEBALL TEAM
By Norman Raike

Our family, consisting of nine children, was living in the lower Bucks County town of Fallsington, Pa., when my mother died unexpectedly. My father was working as a farm laborer at the time and did not have the wherewithal to support and care for us. Most of my siblings were farmed out to relatives, but my 9-year-old sister and I were shipped off to Tabor Home in January 1929.

Even though living at Tabor with about 80 children was quite different from a family setting, I seem to remember that having all those kids to play with was quite satisfactory and I didn't give it much thought. Sister Lena Beideck was the head matron, and two Sisters, Bertha and Thelma, were in charge of the boys' house.

Children in the first three years of school were home-schooled in the cottage that was located on the grounds and taught by one of the Sisters. After completing third grade, we all went to Sunnyside School, which was located on Lower Bucks Road a mile or so from the Home. Miss Buckman, who retired after accumulating 49 years at Sunnyside, taught all eight grades. Talk about dedication! I do remember going to school with the Seibolds (Walter and Russell), Ted Winkle and Walter Trettin, although they were not all in my class.

All the children had chores, and that was just a fact of life. In the summer there were always vegetables to be weeded, wheat to be harvested, potatoes to be collected in bushel baskets, corn to be husked and hay to be raked, stacked and transferred to the barn in huge wagons. When I reached my 14th birthday, I was anointed as one of the barn boys, responsible for mucking out the horse and cow stables and milking the cows twice a day. I clearly remember my foot being stepped on by a cow I was milking and tumbling into the cow manure ditch behind the row of cows. That was a memorable day, but not one that I want to repeat. One desirable aspect of working at the barn was being able to drive the old Ford tractor in the fields. A lot of kids were envious of the tractor driver.

I was only an average student in academics, and I didn't really have much interest in playing sports on school teams. I did pitch for the Tabor baseball team and can recall several games that I struck out a lot of the opposing hitters.

The Tabor bus would take all the kids to high school in the

morning, but you were on your own to get back home in the evening. Most of us would walk or hitchhike the mile and a half down Route 611.

One of the inflexible rules at Tabor at the time was departing when you reached your 17th birthday. Sister Lena escorted me to the recruiting office of the Civilian Conservation Corps (CCC) and had me sign on for a six-month enlistment at the princely sum of $30 a month plus room and board. I ended up extending for another six months before I was released. As a member of the CCC, I helped build the camp located near Thurmont, Maryland, that was later named Camp David when Dwight Eisenhower became president in the 1950s.

After the war started, I was drafted into the Army Air Corps, from which I was discharged in 1945. After the war, I was asked if I would like to work as the full-time farmer at Tabor. It took me only a second to turn down the request. I got married to my present wife in January 1946 and consider it one of the smartest decisions of my life. She concurs.

Norman arrived at Tabor with his older sister Catherine in January 1929 and left 10 years later at the age of 17. He lives in New Hope, Pa., with his wife Elinor.

CROWING ROOSTERS WOULD WAKE ME UP
By Rudolph Krause

My family was living in Philadelphia in the 1920s when the Depression hit. Suddenly, there were no jobs and no money. The decision was made to send me off to Tabor Home in Doylestown, Pa. I was 6 years old and the eldest of three children. My younger brother Walter and sister Alvina would follow me to the Home at a later date.

I remember arriving by car and feeling quite leery of this new and strange place that I would call home for the next eight years. It took me about two weeks to learn the routine and adjust to my new environment. After that initial "break-in" period, I rather enjoyed my childhood at Tabor. There were plenty of kids to play with, and I remember most of us got along quite well. Although we would wrestle with one another, I never remember a fistfight during my years at the Home. Most of our spare time was spent playing sports such as football, basketball and baseball. The food was good, and there was always enough to eat.

Living in any institution requires change, and Tabor was no different. One unusual aspect of growing up there was the sharing of clothes. Since we received a lot of donated clothes, it was common for the Sisters to assist the younger kids in selecting their wardrobe from the available pile. Very few Tabor kids established a strong sense of ownership about what they wore.

There were two sleeping rooms in the boys' dormitory. The larger room was for the younger children and could sleep about 25 kids. The back room, which housed the older boys, was adjacent to the chicken yard, and crowing roosters would wake me up in the morning. All the children ate their three meals in the girls' house, and a large bell at the main door announced when it was time to dine.

In the 1930s, the first few grades of elementary school were conducted at the cottage located right on the grounds. I then attended Castle Valley for the middle years and finished up at Edison for the seventh and eighth grades. I always liked school and enjoyed learning. Education was deemed quite important at Tabor, and study hall was mandatory. The "duty" Sister was available for help if any child needed it to complete his or her homework.

Sister Lena Beideck was the head administrator, and she and her staff did their best to raise the 80 or so children that were placed in her care. I felt we were treated well. When we violated the rules, we were punished with a slap on the hand or the loss of privileges. We were kept busy with chores such as harvesting hay and wheat in the summer, as well as weeding the truck patch or picking up potatoes on the 17-acre field. Some of the boys were selected to assist the tenant farmer with the barn work, including milking the cows by hand twice a day. I was one of the "lucky" ones that was picked.

We could earn money by picking fruit at the local agricultural college that was located about three miles from the Home. We also attended their football and basketball games. We thought nothing of walking the six mile round trip to Farm School.

Just after I finished ninth grade at Doylestown High School, I was informed that I would be leaving Tabor and returning to Philadelphia to live with my parents. I was not pleased with the decision, as I wanted to graduate from Doylestown High. I transferred to Central High School in Philly, where my family lived, and graduated just before World War II.

I was drafted into the Army when I was 19 and ended up in France just hours after D-Day. I had my fill of combat and returned to my hometown after the war.

After two wives and two children, I ended up sending my son Richard to Tabor Home in 1961, when I found I could not support him. He graduated from Central Bucks High School, served in Viet Nam and has turned out to be a person I am very proud of. I think Tabor was the best thing that could have happened to him.

An interesting aside. My daughter Kathleen was married on the Tabor Home grounds, because she thought it was such a beautiful location for a wedding. I am grateful to Sister Wilma for allowing the event to take place.

Rudolph Krause came to Tabor at age 6 and remained there for about eight years. His brother Walter and sister Alvina followed him there. When retired, he lived first with his daughter Kathleen in Philadelphia and then with his son Richard in Fort Lauderdale, Fla. Rudi passed away in July 2005.

MY FIRST DAY AT TABOR HOME
By Genevieve Friel Barrett

My brother Charles and I were in foster care from the time I was 1 year old and he was 3. We lived in Perkasie, Pa., and I believe our foster parent's name was Krause.

Early one morning when I was 5, Mrs. Krause flipped the switch, and the bright light from the overhead fixture flooded my room. "Put on these new clothes, Genny. You will be going somewhere special today," she said as she placed the clothes on the foot of my bed. Then she left the room. I sat up and gazed at the plaid dress and the burgundy-colored oxfords.

After breakfast we got into the car and as we were traveling along the Pennsylvania Turnpike, I remembered a trip we'd taken about three months earlier when my brother sat in the back seat with me. It was on that trip that Mrs. Krause had taken my brother into a tall brick building and had returned to the car, alone. I wondered where my brother was and where I was going today.

Suddenly, a stately black iron fence with a wide gate in the middle came into view. Mr. Krause made a right turn and we drove through the gate. A concrete driveway curved right and then encircled a three-story house. The car came to a halt by the front porch.

As Mrs. Krause and I stood on the porch waiting for someone to answer the doorbell, I thought I'd never seen such a fine house. I closed my eyes and heard a voice say: "Welcome, little child. Please come in. My strong walls will protect you from blizzards and such. Once inside you will surely find happiness."

A woman answered the door, and we stepped into a wide entry hall with large black and white linoleum squares on the floor. To the left, a wooden stairway curved toward the right. Actually, the woman who answered the door was Sister Lena, a Lutheran deaconess, and the place was Tabor Home for Children.

From the entry we passed through an opening and entered a large dining room. Sister Lena told me to sit in a chair as she and Mrs. Krause went into an office and shut the door.

Suddenly I closed my eyes and heard a voice from across the room say: "Come on over here. I am the happy stairway. Children climb up and down my steps everyday. The rule of the house is that children are not supposed to use the stairway in the grand entry hall."

I hurried across the room, climbed the crooked stairway and found myself in a hall. First I turned right, then left, and there I was at the top of the grand stairway. Halfway down the banister, my glee changed to bewilderment as I heard a loud "Bong! Bong!" from behind me. After I came to a stop, I looked up and saw a grandfather clock in an alcove midway up the stairway.

"Oh, it was just a clock," I said, and then went up the stairway as though I were the lady of the house. A series of stairways and hallways spiraled from the first to the third floor. Soon I was at the base of the stairway leading to the third floor, and I heard a voice say, "Come on up and I'll show you your bedroom."

In the room were six white enameled iron beds with white crinkled cotton spreads. I lay down on a bed where the ceiling sloped above.

"Oh, I shall be so happy and cozy here," I said. Suddenly, remembering that I was supposed to be waiting in that chair outside the office, I hurried downstairs as fast as I could. As I stood in the entry hall at the base of the stairs, Sister Lena came in from outside and said, "Oh, there you are. Your foster parents had to leave without telling you goodbye."

Pointing toward the back door, she said, "Go outside with the other children until the dinner bell rings." Before I reached the door, the bell rang and children began coming inside.

"It can't be, but I think ... yes, it is," I shouted as my eyes met those of my brother. We hurried toward each other.

"I haven't seen you since the time Mrs. Krause left me at the hospital," he said.

"Why did she take you there?" I asked.

"I don't know," he replied. And neither of us ever knew why.

He led me through a wide archway to the smaller dining room where the younger children ate. We couldn't sit together, because the boys sat at a separate table from the girls. The warm casserole of meat and macaroni was delicious, but I could hardly swallow my food. I kept smiling at my brother.

Genevieve came to Tabor in 1933 at the age of 5 along with her brother Charles, who was three years older. They remained there until 1942. Charles Friel died in January 2001, and Genevieve presently resides in Beaumont, Texas.

LIVING AT TABOR WASN'T EASY
By Walter (Lefty) Seibold

For the first 12 years of my life, I was shuffled around, boarding with six different relatives in and around the Philadelphia area. I was 12 years old when my younger brother Russell and younger sister Dorothy were all sent to Tabor Home. Russell was 18 months my junior and Dorothy was three years younger. Our parents were physically separated, but they weren't divorced. This arrangement was fairly common in the 1930s.

The first few days at Tabor were horrible. I felt like a lonely, cast-out human being. As I gradually made friends things got a little better, but I must say that living at Tabor wasn't easy. Some of the things I remember were stealing watermelons at Burpee's Farm and getting caught by Sister Lena on the roof of the girls' house after dark.

Sunnyside School was a one-room schoolhouse where the younger Tabor children would go to school. I remember that I didn't learn a thing at that school. I do recall that we often were served sandwiches with green bologna. I believe it was donated and the expiration date (which did not exist) was way overdue. During the Depression, society wasn't so picky. I then went to Edison school at age 14.

About 1936 my parents reunited, and they pulled us out of Tabor for good. I made some good friends there, including Fred Strowig and Harry (Skinny) Clark, with whom I served in the Merchant Marine. I am not sure if I developed a strong work ethic at Tabor, but I know it has helped me during my lifetime.

I got married before the war and then joined the U.S. Navy in 1942, stationed at Newport, R.I.

Lefty Seibold came to Tabor in 1933 with his brother Russell and sister Dorothy, and left three years later. He joined the Merchant Marines in 1938 and the U.S. Navy in 1942. In recent years he lived in Willow Grove, Pa. Lefty died in September 2005.

MY FAVORITE HYMN IS STILL "O ZION HASTE"
By Dorothy Seibold Carter

Intellectually, I realize that it has been more than 70 years since the Seibold clan came to Tabor Home, but some memories remain quite clear. It was during the Depression and times were quite hard for many families. Our parents could not keep the family together financially, and they ended up separating but were not divorced. Brothers, Walter and Russell, and I had been "farmed out" with relatives for several years before we all got back together at Tabor. I had been staying with an aunt in Elkins Park, Pa., just prior to going to the Home.

Sister Lena Beideck was in charge at the time, and Sister Wilma Loehrig was the supervisor in the girls' house. Apparently, the girls' dorm was the old Fretz mansion before they sold the property to Tabor Home, and the boys' dormitory was the carriage house that had been refitted. I still remember the beautifully curved banisters that connected the first two floors in the mansion. It was rather dangerous to slide down them, but occasionally we would ignore the rules and take our lives into our own hands.

One remembrance that brings a smile to my face was the action of some of the boys when vegetables were served that was not to their liking. They would secretly put the hated parsnip or brussels sprout into their pocket and make a face as though they had consumed it.

In my mind's eye I can also see myself standing at the main gate with the huge black rod-iron fence spelling out TABOR HOME FOR CHILDREN, waiting for my mother or father to visit on Sunday. Sadly, some of the children never got visitors, and they had to be envious of the lucky ones that did.

Lutheran sisters supervised the Home, and there was definitely a religious value system that was instilled. We would pray before each meal and have services after evening meal consisting of prayers and hymns. It was not long before one knew most of the hymns by heart. To this day, "O Zion Haste" remains my favorite hymn and the one I would select to sing when my birthday, December 18, rolled around. I can still see Sister Lena's dog sitting on her lap during evening services.

I know every Tabor kid had his or her favorite holiday, and mine was May Day. It occurred on the third Saturday in May each year, and the public was invited to share in the festivities. There were booths selling all sorts of things that today would be for sale at a flea market. The ladies of the Lutheran Church would put on a meal for a token charge, and the kids would put on a play or other entertainment. I remember Russell playing the role of Doctor Foster one year. It was quite entertaining.

When school started Walter went off to Edison, and Russell and I went to a one-room schoolhouse called Sunnyside. Miss Buckman was the school "marm" and she taught all six grades. It seemed like it was about two miles from Tabor, and we walked to school when the weather was good but rode the school bus during the winter. A girl my age may not be the best judge of distance but it seemed quite far at the time.

One additional memory was the love we had for molasses bread. It was served at two meals, and we used it for bartering. I believe we got eggs about once a week, so it was quite special when they were served.

It was a glorious day in 1936 when our parents reunited our family, but my memories of my days at Tabor Home will live in my mind forever.

Dorothy Seibold came to Tabor with her two older brothers in 1933 and remained there for only three years. She married Elmer Carter in 1947 and presently lives in Marlton, N.J.

THE LIFE OF A NEW KID WAS THE PITS
By Thomas d'Arcy

My parents divorced shortly after my brother Bill was born. The Depression years were too hard financially for our mother to support us. So in 1932 we made the trip from Philadelphia to Doylestown for a permanent home. We had lived in Cuba for about three years and for a short period of time in New York City, but my memory of those years is very hazy.

As a relatively sensitive 5-year-old boy, I was not ready for the harsh reality of growing up with 40 other boys. The little kids' bedroom slept more than 20 children. Each child was expected to make his bed, dress himself and ensure his dirty clothes got washed. Those initial days were quite traumatic, and I spent a lot of time crying and feeling very lonely. It was clearly the worst time of my life. In contrast, Bill adjusted better to the group environment and seemed to have a tougher demeanor during the period when getting beaten up by the older boys was a rite of passage. In short order, when we both learned how to fight, the bullying essentially stopped. Being raised without parents or nurturing certainly affects one's personality, but I guess individuals react to stress in different ways.

I felt an obligation to look after my brother and vice versa. We took care of one another in the 11 years we were at Tabor. Both of us were pretty good athletes, and there was ample opportunity to hone one's skills on the athletic fields. I lettered in football, baseball and track at Doylestown High.

Because my mother could not afford the required fees at Tabor for Bill and me, she was always in Sister Lena's doghouse. She would avoid Sister Lena on Sundays by meeting us in the woods, not wanting a confrontation over money.

As I got older, I was the designated "barn guy" whose job it was to milk the cows, clean out the stalls and do the countless other tasks that Harry (Boog) Burmeister had lined up. There were some perks that went along with the position, but the downside was it was a seven-day-a-week task and a farmer's job is never done. I can clearly remember looking down the rows of potatoes on the 17-acre field and thinking it would take an eternity to weed all these potato plants.

As I look back on events from more than 50 years ago, I have a mixture of feelings. There are many pleasant memories such as

Burpee's orchard, our cherry trees, Confirmation Day, sledding and Sunnyside's one room schoolhouse. I also fondly remember Sister Lena and her dogs, Donut Day, the Doylestown Fair, the woods, fishing, trapping skunks, Christmas with small stockings of candy, swimming, throw-up-and-tackle games, playing peggy, kick the can and Halloween. Other positive remembrances were walking from school in the snow, Friday's bath ritual, marbles, silent movies and then talkies. I could go on and on.

The circumstances surrounding my leaving Tabor at the age of 16 were curious. During a rally in which we were collecting cans and food for the war effort, I ran outside during evening prayers. Sister Wilma told me to keep on going, back to my mother. The next day Billy and I left the Home for good.

I worked on a dairy farm for a year before I joined the ground infantry and later transferred to the 82nd airborne paratroopers. I got out in 1948, remarried and eventually owned my own business. I had some health problems through the years, but I feel very healthy now and cherish each day. My poem, "God's Country," says it all!

God's Country
By Thomas d'Arcy

I love the air and sunshine, the open fields of grain.
The smell of earth, the hay and corn, mistflowers, wind and rain.
Those peaceful skies and rolling hills, the fleecy clouds above,
The little town and red schoolhouse are also things I love.
Where everyone is happy, the rich, the poor, the famed,
Out where a friend is more than merely just a name.
Away from crowds, the noise and smoke, which city folks thrive on.
I'd rather live in God's Country, away out on a farm.

Tom came to Tabor in 1932 at the age of 5 along with his 4-year-old brother Bill. They remained there for 11 years. Bill died of a heart attack when he was 58 years old. Tom presently lives in Cocoa, Fla., with his wife Joan.

THE BEST OF TIMES, THE WORST OF TIMES
By Bill Beck

Since the time I can remember, it seems I had always lived at Tabor. I know my brother George came there with me, but only because I was told that fact later in life. My sister Daisy came later, but those details are quite hazy. I do remember being taken to the boys' dormitory by Sister Mary, shortly after I arrived. At 3 years old, one's analytical skills are not well developed, so I don't recall being scared or homesick or anything like that.

Childhood seemed quite normal, and there were more than a few adventures while growing up. The woods that were adjacent to the buildings were ideal for young boys. It gave us opportunities to build huts, explore, hike and play war games. I still remember the fun I had sledding down the wagon path or riding on the V-shaped plow when Boog Burmeister, the farmer, plowed the snow off the sidewalks and driveways. Some kids raised rabbits, and others shot at birds and squirrels with "slappies." I don't mean to imply that we never got into trouble. We did our share of picking and eating green apples from the orchard or stealing melons from Burpee's Farm and disappearing into the woods to consume the ill-gotten gains. But, all in all, a pretty ideal place to spend a childhood.

Just about every kid at Tabor loved Sister Lena Beideck, the headmistress. She seemed to know just when to show concern or say a kind word or call someone into her office and give a small present or some money for a special treat. It was a big disappointment for me when Sister Wilma Loehrig replaced her in 1942.

When I was in high school I was assigned chores at the barn, shoveling cow manure among other tasks. One day, when I was supposed to be working at the barn, I decided to take off for Philadelphia with friends from the local gas station. Unfortunately for me, I got caught, and my transgression was reported to Sister Wilma. She quickly relayed to me the message, "If you don't like it here, do us all a favor and leave." Having no great love for high school and seeing little success remaining at Tabor, I decided to take her at her word. The same day I packed up what little worldly possessions I had (two shirts, a pair of trousers and a sweater), and moved into the gas station.

Fortune smiled on me in the form of Pop Childs, the school

janitor. He saw my plight and invited me to live in his trailer park. As soon as I turned 18 years old, I joined the Navy and commenced learning about the real world.

My final thoughts are that I think Sister Wilma really ruined it at Tabor for the majority of the children that lived there. I also think I had an exceptional childhood at Tabor, and I was a lot better off than staying home with my father.

Bill was brought to Tabor Home when he was about 3 years old. He left 14 years later in 1947. His older brother and sister, George and Daisy, also lived there. He presently resides in Toano, Va.

LIFE WAS NOT A BOWL OF CHERRIES
By Daisy Beck

I was living with a foster family in Philadelphia just before I was sent to Tabor Home in the late 1930s. My mother worked for a member of the Tabor board of directors, a Walter Desrouth.

I have two distinct memories about my initial day at the Home. The large buildings were overwhelming as the two women from the Lutheran Bureau escorted me through those imposing iron gates with the large letters, "TABOR HOME FOR CHILDREN." Later in the day I saw both my brothers, George and Bill, but they pretended not to know me. Apparently, it was not macho to acknowledge that they had a sister.

In looking back at my days at Tabor, I realize that I learned a lot of useful skills such as cooking, laundering clothes, mending and gardening. My fondest memories are how enjoyable the holidays were at Tabor. Christmas, May Day and Easter were my favorites. May Day was especially memorable with all the booths selling wares; alumni were always in attendance, and the whole community seemed very supportive of the children. You felt special.

The last few weeks at Tabor would not make the highlight film. I was 15 years old and sitting at the end of Sister Wilma's table at supper. She was about to make an announcement when I heard a plate fall to the floor and I turned my head to see what the commotion was about. Apparently she thought I was laughing at her, and she proceeded to walk to the end of the table and smacked me across the face. In my surprise and disbelief, I reacted and returned the favor, as a collective gasp came from the entire dining room. The immediate response was a stern shout from Sister Wilma, "Pack your bags and leave, now."

About an hour later with bags in hand, I was met at the front door and told, "Get back to your room. You can't leave until I contact your mother." Within the week my mother was contacted and my Tabor days were over.

Years later I visited Tabor and ran into Sister Wilma. She was so sweet to me I felt like throwing up.

Daisy came to Tabor at about the age of 6. She remained there until she was 15. Her older brother George and her younger brother Bill were already residents when she arrived. Daisy presently lives in Philadelphia.

DO YOU KNOW HOW TO FIGHT, NEW KID?
By Charles Frankenfield

Before coming to Tabor Home I lived in Horsham, Pa., with my grandparents, who were in their 70s, and my 15-year-old uncle. I spent a lot of time hanging around WPA workers who were building roads near my house. I picked up a lot of their colorful language that, as a small child, I thought was acceptable English. When they moved into an old folk's home, I was sent to Tabor.

One of my earliest memories was how the pecking order was established. The first question I was asked on my very first day was "Do you know how to fight, new kid?" After getting beat up by most of the bigger boys, I learned where I fit into the organization. Despite the rather harsh indoctrination, I made friends quickly and adjusted fairly easily to the new survival ground rules.

The two matrons in charge of the boys' dormitory were Sister Helma and Sister Sophie. Neither would be confused with Mary Poppins. They were strict disciplinarians and were not very impressed with a 5-year-old who spoke salty language that one might expect from the mouth of a seagoing sailor. Within the first month I got into trouble with Sister Helma for using my bed like a trampoline. I was living in the front dorm that housed 20-plus younger boys. I later expressed my general frustration by shouting expletives after several of the older kids yanked my pillow from under my head, just as Sister was entering the room. Those incidents resulted in my being transferred to the back room, which housed the older boys, for a little "tough love" discipline.

One of the backroom boys was Bob Ralston, who worked at the barn and happened to be a varsity football player for the high school. Several of my newly acquired roommates informed me that his name was Horse S___ Ralston and that was how I was to address him. That evening I greeted Ralston with his proper nickname and was immediately given a physical reprimand accompanied by the phrase, "You Humpty Dumpty!" The nickname stuck, and for the next 12 years I was known as Humpty Frankenfield. To this day, I am occasionally addressed by old acquaintances as Humpty.

As a youngster I was not the most diligent of workers, especially if the task was something like picking up potatoes in the

17-acre field. One time the hired farmer, Harry Burmeister, became exasperated with my obvious goofing off and threatened to "root me in the butt" if I didn't start picking up my share of spuds. I chose to duck into the weeds rather than work. In short order, Harry discovered my hiding place and hurried over to make good his threat. I jumped up and ran away while shouting, "You #*%*#! You'll never catch me." He ignored me, and I was quite smug about beating the system.

Within the year I was in the back room picking something off the floor when I felt a sharp pain in my posterior and felt myself literally flying over my bed and landing unceremoniously in a heap on the bedroom floor. Amid the gales of laughter from everyone in the room, I saw Harry Burmeister pointing at me and saying, "I caught you, didn't I?"

Charlie Frankenfield was 5 years old when he entered Tabor Home in 1933. His siblings, John, Clara and Mary, were already living there. He remained at Tabor Home until he was drafted into the Navy in 1945 after graduating from Doylestown High School. He was stationed in the Aleutian Islands, which are located in Alaska. Until his death on November 6, 2006, Charlie lived in Doylestown with his wife Ruth.

TO THIS DAY I CANNOT STAND
THE TASTE OF GARLIC
By Arlene Amend

My earliest memory was the day my mother delivered me to Tabor Home. I clearly remember the impressive staircase in the girls' house and waving goodbye to my mother from the steps. Tabor seemed like a step up from the Salvation Army-run home in Philadelphia where I had spent the prior two years. My assigned room was on the third floor with five or six other girls. Sliding down the long, curved banister to the first floor is a memory still lodged in my head after 60 years.

My general impression was that of living in a loving atmosphere and being very fond of Sister Lena Beideck. My background of institutional-living from the age of 3 may have tempered this impression. Specific memories that stand out were:

- Being impressed with the automatic potato peeler in the kitchen. The ability of a machine to remove skins so efficiently seemed nothing short of miraculous to me.

- Remembering the day that Franklin Roosevelt died. I had kitchen duty when his death was announced in April 1945.

- Admiring the portrait of Sister Lena with children and Jesus Christ in the background. I thought it was quite large and a remarkable likeness of someone we all loved and admired. (Seeing it recently I was disappointed by its small size and faded background.)

- Staring in awe of the monstrous bull in the end stall in the barn along with the rest of the herd of milking cows. In those days we drank unpasteurized milk directly from the hand-milked cows. The cream that rose to the top was scooped off and made into butter. Each spring when the cows were permitted to graze in the pastures, the unmistakable taste of garlic permeated the milk. To this day I cannot stand the taste of garlic.

- Buying packs of seeds at Burpees and planting victory gardens in plots near the woods. Seeds were only a nickel a pack, and the glorious pictures, which were depicted on the package, set a standard that was seldom reached by the novice planters.

- Ice-skating at the "rocks" or at a nearby pond in the winter and being amused when a boy occasionally penetrated the thin ice and walked home wet and cold.
- Being impressed with the elementary principal, Paul Kutz, because he let me ring the bell that announced school was beginning or ending.
- Picking up potatoes in the 17-acre field with the rest of the kids at Tabor. The rows seemed so long you never thought you would get all the potatoes picked up.

I look back with fond memories regarding Tabor Home and regretted moving to Miami to live with Mother in 1945. I learned self-discipline due to the structured lifestyle we lived. Daily study hall and monthly letters to my mother were just two examples of mandatory requirements that set a fine standard for mature living.

Arlene Amend was 6 years old when she came to Tabor Home in 1937. She stayed through eighth grade and left in 1945 to live with her mother and stepfather. She resides in North Carolina and Florida with her husband Jim.

WANTED: SUMMER CAMP COUNSELOR.
PAY: $25/Month
By George Breitling

I was hired by Dr. Walter McKinney to work at Tabor Home as a summer counselor. The only thing I knew before I reported for duty was that it was a home for children from broken families, and I was hired to keep the boys busy with physical activities including sports and some farm work. I was also expected to be a role model, even though I was only several years older than some of my charges.

As soon as I arrived, I fell ill with some sort of virus and was bed-ridden for the first week on the job. I am not too sure how pleased Sister Lena was to have to nurse me back to health my very first week, but she never indicated any disappointment. Stuff happens!

I don't think I had any specific expectations when I reported in for work at Tabor Home. I was certainly struck by the beauty of Bucks County and the surrounding countryside. There were two other college kids hired with me the first year, but for some reason I was the only one that signed on for the subsequent two years.

The tasking was clear-cut. When there was farm work to accomplish, we rounded up the usual suspects and helped their efforts with the farmer, Harry J. Berger, and his right-hand man, Harry (Boog) Burmeister. There was the normal complaining but, by and large, every one pitched in until the job was done.

Sister Lena Beideck was the head matron, and three other sisters assisted her. I was quite impressed with the skills of Sister Lena in running such a complex organization. Virtually all the children loved her, respected her wishes and hated to disappoint her. She was lovable and capable, traits that are not universal in supervisors the world over.

Dr. McKinney, president of the Tabor Home board, was also a memorable person. Each summer he would load up the Tabor bus with children and transport them to Lankenau Hospital in Philadelphia, where he would remove their tonsils. It was never clear to me how one got on the list.

In September he invited all the counselors to spend a week at his house in Ocean City. He had just the right touch of giving us free rein during the day and hosting us in his gracious style in the evening. He was quite remarkable.

The longer I spent at Tabor Home the more I found out about the area. I was especially impressed with the Bucks County Playhouse and their offerings. I attended several of their plays during my evenings off duty.

My overall impression of my three summers at Tabor was that I helped supervise some pretty good kids with a positive male influence. The fact that I returned for two more years should speak for itself regarding my experience. I developed a real affection and respect for Tabor Home, and I have it to this day.

George Breitling was a college student when he was hired to work as a camp counselor in the summer of 1937 and two subsequent summers. After graduating from Temple University in 1940, he was drafted into the Army the following year. He presently lives in Newton Square, Pa.

Chapter Three - The 1940s

TABOR BOY MAKES GOOD
By Jake Highton

Memory is faulty. It often fails us about recent events let alone after decades. So I cannot guarantee that these memoirs are absolutely factual. But they are the truth as I recall those days so long ago.

My first night at Tabor Home was anguishing, an introduction to the bitter realities of life. I was 4½ when I arrived at the Home in the summer of 1935. I was not an orphan. My mother lived in New York City where I was born January 14, 1931, and my father in Doylestown, about one mile north of Tabor on Route 611. The incident is emblazoned on my memory. I was in the big bedroom of the boys' dormitory that first night. I cuddled a doll, as young kids are wont to do. I think it was a Mickey Mouse doll. Whatever. It was my only friend so naturally I clung to it. Suddenly, one of the older boys grabbed the doll and began tossing it around to other boys. I was devastated.

My next memory was painful too. But this time it was my fault. Outside the boys' dorm we had a sandbox near a chain link fence separating it from the swimming pool. I was about 5 or 6, playing with a toy steam shovel that I think belonged to Billy Beck. I broke the shovel. When the owner confronted me as the likely perpetrator, I lied. I said I was not responsible. My first lie still is embedded in my memory.

My next unhappy memory came a year or so later. It was the end of my first grade at Doylestown Township Elementary School about a mile south of Tabor. Every Tabor kid who excelled at school that year was rewarded with a bag of candy. I, who had excelled, was overlooked. I can still see myself crying on the front porch – under the big dinner bell of the administration building – because I was not rewarded as I should have been. But Sister Lena Beideck, gentle and lovable Tabor administrator, rectified the oversight. All was well that ended well.

I recall sitting through that first grade year, terrified every day that the teacher would see the big scratch on my desk, blame it on me and give me a licking. Fortunately, my worst fears never came to pass. It was also fortune, because I had not scratched the desk.

Another memory from the age of 5 or 6. We kids would take a nap after lunch in the boys' playroom, sleeping on a rug. I recall, too, as a youngster that sometimes we had fistfights. A bigger kid

40

once gave me a black eye. But fighting was not my style. I was not a brawler.

The most terrifying incident to happen to me occurred in the long playroom near the front of the boys' building. Each of us had a footlocker where we stored our gear: roller and ice skates, balls, bat and glove, football and helmet. The terror: one day a bigger kid coaxed me into my locker, slammed the lid and sat on it. The claustrophobia was overwhelming. I frantically banged on the lid for what seemed like an eternity. Finally, the kid let me out. My relief was inexpressible.

We used to line up at the head of the walkway, which ran from the main building to the front gate, to walk to elementary school. I recall as a youngster of 7 or 8 uttering some mild curse word as we waited one day to start to school. I was horrified, quickly clamping my hand over my mouth. I really was a puritanical kid not given to using "bad language." To this day I do not swear except in quoting in a classroom or what someone said. It's not that I am puritanical anymore. No, it's just that I came to love the English language. I refuse to debase it. A friend and colleague of mine at the University of Nevada, Reno, where I teach, has an IQ about 50 points higher than mine. Yet he seems incapable of speaking a sentence without using three swear words. It ill becomes him. Another thing I recall from the walk to school: It always puzzled me to see the moon still in the sky while the sun was shining. To this day I know little about science.

In third grade I felt my first pangs of puppy love. The girl's name was Rachel. I don't remember whether she was one of the several girls in school who wore the Mennonite hair covering.

Mathematics was hardly my forte. But I recall winning a math prize in seventh or eighth grade. I also must have been a popular kid, because I was elected president of the seventh grade class. As, indeed, I must have been popular in high school, because I was elected junior class president. (Class elections are usually based on popularity instead of issues as in political campaigns.)

In grammar school I got the nickname Jake. (My real name is Robert Donald Highton.) Jake stuck. Eventually, no one who knew me called me Bob except my mother. She remarked one day when I went to New York on vacation: "Oh, Bob, I gave you a good Christian name and you call yourself Jake." The fact is I am Jake. Period. Indeed, many friends and acquaintances today think Jake is my real name.

Here is how I became Jake. Tabor Home had an older kid named Jacob Fetzer. He was dark-complexioned as I am, he had a hot temper as I did and he loved the New York Yankees as I did. One day a Tabor kid, seeing me approach, remarked: "Here comes little Jake." Soon all the kids and even the teachers began calling me Jake. When I went to Doylestown High School, the kids there also began calling me Jake. Before long the teachers did too. When I left Tabor and enrolled at Penn State I could have dropped Jake, because just a handful of students there knew me. But, no, I had become Jake. During the summer I wrote sports for the Doylestown Intelligencer and began using the byline Jake Highton. The Intelligencer sports editor, Russ Thomas, became fond of me. Whatever modest honors came to me after I left Tabor, Thomas would write an item to the effect that "Tabor Home boy makes good." (No Tabor kid who remained at Tabor through high school had ever graduated from college, and a few over the years had questionable reputations.)

In seventh grade I discovered the wonder of girls. I was infatuated with Arlene Amend, a tall, attractive, personable and intelligent Tabor girl. About a year later she left Tabor. I was crushed. And, like so many kids, I thought I would never fall in love again. It took me a long time to realize that I would never see her again. I remember saying to Sister Wilma Loehrig, who had succeeded Sister Lena, that someday I would marry Arlene. She replied, cruelly I thought: "You almost never marry your first love." Shattering. But she was right.

I remember kissing Arlene on the back steps of the girls' dorm. Indeed, I recall sneaking from the boys' dorm late at night, creeping up the back steps to her room to kiss and cuddle. Creeping up and down the steps, stealthily opening and closing doors, carried the pulse-pounding danger of being caught. And, yes, I carved her initials in a beech tree in the Tabor woods. The last time I was at Tabor, decades ago, I looked up that tree. The carving wounds were widened and blackened with age. But the heart and arrow were there. And so was "J.H. loves A.A."

It was in grammar school that I began a lifelong love of sports. I played on the grade school football team, although I don't remember what position. We played a home-and-home series with Chalfont. After we lost one of the games I wept inconsolably. I was a fiery competitor who could not stand losing.

Games. I recall playing an all-star baseball board game on top of the concrete water tank in the Tabor woods. You spun a dial, landing on spaces to tell whether you got a hit or made an out. A slugger like Babe Ruth would have a broad band for a home run. Wee Willie Keeler, a "hit 'em where they ain't" singles hitter, would have no band for a home run. And wire ball. We would toss the ball up to wires about 10 feet above us. If the ball missed the wires, it was an out. If you hit one wire it was a single. I forget exactly how we scored. During the game, at my turn to bat, I would run down every player in the Yankee lineup. And kick the can. And rolling a rubber ball up and down the roof of a small storage shed near the laundry room. The laundry also served as the infirmary where kids with communicable diseases were isolated. And the joy of tossing around the baseball for the first time of the year, sometime in late February or early March, even before all the snow had melted. I used to shag fly balls hit by older kids when I was about 10. Flattery got them everywhere. They would say: "Boy, that Jake runs like a deer!" Speaking of running. Once, when I was about 7, I burst out running about 25 yards at top speed from pure animal joy – a delight in being alive.

I fancied myself an athlete although I weighed a mere 134 pounds. At Doylestown High School I was on the track team, high jumping and running a leg on the mile relay team. I was also the first team right end on the football squad, playing both offense and defense as we did in the late 1940s. But I realized years later that I was neither heavy enough nor good enough to play on one of the far superior football teams in Philadelphia or some of the Main Line teams. Still, I felt that I should have been a starter on the Doylestown High basketball team, because the fifth guy was weak. But I had not played basketball in grammar school so I did not go out for the team.

I also realized years later that I had no natural athletic talent. All I had was guts. I frequently blocked or brushed past opponents who outweighed me by 40 pounds. Great Britain's General Wellington said, "The battle of Waterloo was won on the playing fields of Eton." Well, I won no battles except sometimes against opposing tackles. But those battles were won on Tabor Home's front lawn. We called the game bone crusher. It was one Tabor kid against another. You had four downs to go 10 yards for a touchdown. You could run or throw yourself a pass. I recall playing in the rain one day, the lawn muddy and our clothes dirty.

I think my bone-crushing foe was Eddie Merkel. Anyway, the lawn game toughened me, enabling me to play high school football despite my pitifully light weight.

Playing football two years at Doylestown High, I scored just twice, once recovering a fumble in the end zone against Quakertown, and another time on a long pass and run in a game against Souderton when everyone was scoring because we won 51-7. In my senior year we were something like 6-0 and the Philadelphia Bulletin – or was it the Inquirer? – gave the team a big write-up. Mistake. We lost two or three of our next games including the big, big Thanksgiving Day game against archrival Lansdale.

Actually, my greatest feat in an inglorious football career was a defensive gem, as the sports writers say. It was a turning point of a game with Ambler. (I was chagrined that the play was not even mentioned in the Doylestown Intelligencer.) Ambler was unbeaten behind the speedy running back Earl Mundell. DHS pulled off a big upset, something like 13-6. In the second half, Mundell came streaking around his left end behind two blockers. I tripped up both protectors with a full body-block and tackled the ball carrier. Mundell fumbled, and we recovered the ball on their 35-yard line. The winning touchdown was scored after the turnover. Which reminds me of one of my teachers in high school, math instructor Forrest Sowers. The week before games he would scrawl on his blackboard exhortations like: "Make the Quakers quake," or, "Land on Lansdale."

And baseball. We played often on the Tabor ball field after supper. Once I was shagging fly balls in the field that served as the outfield. A kid hit a ball over my head so far, in fact, that the ball rolled all the way into the ditch along Route 611. Retrieving the ball, I was amazed to find a $10 bill in the ditch. It paid my way to Boy Scout camp for a week. (Camp Ockanickon was about 15 miles from Tabor.) We Tabor kids were poor, so that was finding "manna" from heaven.

I once went to a Sunday doubleheader of the Philadelphia A's hosting the New York Yankees. I took the Philadelphia Transit Company bus to the Olney subway station, got off at Lehigh Avenue and walked to Shibe Park. During the game I had precious little money for sodas and hotdogs. Indeed, I had to beg money to get home. But I was happy: I had seen my beloved Joe DiMaggio play. (And how it hurt me to hear Philly fans boo him.)

44

Ah, sports. Often the salvation of Tabor kids. It became a ritual in the fall to walk the roughly two miles down the back road to Farm School for Saturday football games. (The games were free.) The Farm School football team had so few players there might be just two or three players sitting on the bench. Indeed, one Farm School player joined the two-man band at halftime to beat the bass drum. The Farmers used the single-wing then in vogue. I can still hear the quarterback, Abbie Spinola, barking out the signals: "18-88-91-4, 5, 4 ..." Oh, and we Tabor kids would steal apples from the Farm School orchard on the way to the games.

The driveways around the dorms and administration building were wonderful roller skating "rinks." In the winter they made fine sledding paths. After particularly heavy snowfalls, you could sled across Route 611, cross in front of the barn to the meadow and, if lucky, sled all the way to the millrace, as we called the creek area. I recall a night sitting on a sled near the flagpole talking with a girl who I wished had been Arlene. Even so, it was a starry night, a romantic night, a night such as Shakespeare described in the fifth act of "The Merchant of Venice."

Although my heart belonged to Arlene, my head belonged to Dot Maloney. She was my pal, my buddy. Although she was an attractive blonde, we had no sexual chemistry. But what we had was more important: genuine, deep friendship. Many an evening we would spend hours talking while standing by the concrete wall that separated the back of the boys' dorm from the chicken yard. I don't recall the particulars of any of our conversations, but they were what we thought were profound, what poet Longfellow called "the long, long thoughts" of youth. We did reflect on the misfortune of being a Tabor kid. I certainly thought the Home was a jail, that our fate was cruel. Thus, we would talk about life, the sometimes bitterness of life. I was always a melancholy and unhappy kid. I remember a sophomore classmate of mine at DHS asking me one day: "Why so morose, Jake?" At the time I did not know what the word meant. But he was so right.

Two things I missed most at Tabor Home: lack of love and lack of direction. We felt self-conscious about being Tabor kids. I certainly felt stigmatized, "homeless." I recall that Don McCarthy, tall, blond Adonis on the Doylestown High football team, basketball and baseball star, invited me to his house one weekend. I refused because I had no home to invite him to in return. Stupid, yes. But that is the way I then felt.

One of the problems at the Home was the institutional cooking. Oatmeal and mush was served at breakfast, in cold, flat, unpalatable blobs. To this day I cannot eat oatmeal even if served hot and sugary. Psychological. Spinach the same way. It was cold, stringy, gagging. Even now I cannot eat spinach. But we Tabor kids compensated by sometimes raiding the pantry. Our target: No. 10 cans of fruit. Sometimes we bought a package of sticky buns from a bakery truck for a nickel.

As for direction, I mostly directed myself, although my mother did encourage me to build my vocabulary. And I remember a gift book one of her friends in New York gave me for Christmas in 1947: the complete, illustrated works of Longfellow. That green-covered volume spurred my love of poetry. His verse was so encouraging to a boy: "The heights by great men reached and kept / Were not attained by sudden flight, / But they, while their companions slept, / Were toiling upward in the night." Or: "Lives of great men all remind us / We can make our lives sublime, / And, departing, leave behind us, / Footprints on the sands of time."

I became *un homme serieux* (a serious man), an intellectual if you will, a polemicist, a controversialist, a man bursting with opinions, a man who loved to wrestle with ideas. Eventually, I became more interested in literature and politics than in sports. I became a Man of the Left. I grew more and more angry at U.S. history, U.S. policies, and yearly-by-yearly more radical.

My progress was from a conservative kid to a liberal young man. I first voted in 1956, voting for the Democratic candidate for president, Adlai Stevenson. Then I became the socialist I am today. I am a card-carrying member of the American Civil Liberties Union, the Sierra Club and the Audubon Society – all expressions of my love for civil liberties, the environment and bird watching.

As for intellect, I was spurred by exchanges of letters with my grandfather in New York. He was what was called in those days a freethinker. I was a cross-wearing, down-on-my knees, praying Christian. I used to quote to him from the Bible or poet Walt Whitman. He would write back with cogent arguments against the existence of God and provide atheistic quotations. (He "won" the argument later, although at the time I did not think so.) No wonder in those days I wanted to become a minister. I loved words and I loved to emote. I thought it would be great to speak pearly words every week. And, deep down, I was a ham. But I came to realize that I could not preach about God when I did not believe in God.

The turning point began a couple of years after World War II ended. I had followed the war in the Philadelphia Bulletin. Then, suddenly, the United States was in a cold war with the Soviet Union. No guide to the universe, no God, would permit this. Surely, I thought, the idea of God was absurd. (I later read deeply in history. Anyone who does cannot believe in God.) Then I went away to college and read Thomas Paine's "The Age of Reason." I have been a militant atheist ever since.

Anyway, we Tabor kids went to the Lutheran Church in Doylestown every Sunday on the Tabor bus. The minister was Reverend Repass who spoke with an accent. Kids are great mockers, so naturally we made fun of him. I can still hear myself saying, "FO-teenth," the way he pronounced fourteenth. But I was certainly religious in those days. I remember one Good Friday. The sky was black with storm clouds, the wind blew. I stood on the hill outside the boys' dorm, my arms outstretched as if I were Christ on the cross. When I ran track I was fond of these lines from I Corinthians: "Know ye not that they which run in a race run all, but one receiveth the prize?" One final religious note: Every night at dinner we had a passage read from the Bible. I do not remember if it was the King James Version. I hope so. It is still one of my favorite books.

I had a small calendar on which I had written my four goals in life. The first was to live like Christ. Absurd. Another was to write like Shakespeare. Absurd. Another was to run a four-minute mile. Absurd. I could barely run a mile in five minutes. The fourth goal was at least in the realm of possibility: Write like Red Smith. Smith was my favorite sports writer, crisp and clear, literate and literary. I did become a sports writer but not a Red Smith. (When I reached the Penn State campus, still fancying myself an athlete, I went out for the cross-country team. In a couple of days I realized the State harriers were running five miles just to warm up. I went out for the school paper.)

Oh, yes, then I wanted to be an actor. (Dot Maloney always said I had a wonderful speaking voice.) I recall one Tabor Christmas pageant. I was one of the Wisemen. I still remember one of my singing lines: "Who's knocking there?" I was a terrible singer. The one D that I got in high school was in music. Another time I appeared in a Tabor drama. (We had a stage downstairs in

47

the auditorium of the girls' dorm.) I played a villain. Once, having repossessed a mortgage deed, I placed it in my jacket breast pocket. In the next scene I came on stage with the deed still visible in my pocket. Another character asked me for the deed. My line was: "Do you suppose I carry such important documents around with me?" What mortification!

We kids were often naughty, climbing the big pine near the sandbox to peek into the girls' windows at night. (I recall that with embarrassment.) Another time, a cuddly Tabor twosome, an older boy and girl, wanted to be alone so they started walking toward the dirt road toward Farm School. I insisted on following. Then the big kid hurled a stone at me, causing a gash in my forehead. I got the message – painfully.

I was a serious kid. I recall as a high school senior reading "Hamlet," sitting alone on the parquet floor of the dimly lit Tabor dining room. "Hamlet" sparked a lifelong love for Shakespeare in particular and literature and poetry in general. Literature was always a great consolation in my often unhappy journey through life. My love of the mind was spurred by an Army bull session shortly after I graduated from Penn State in 1953. In college I was so respected by my fraternity brothers that one chap would constantly ask during a discussion: "Isn't that right, Jake?" (As if I were the wise man, the authority.) Anyway, a fellow in my Army outfit, a brilliant guy from New York, was talking learnedly about history, politics, literature and philosophy – about everything it seemed. Suddenly, I had an epiphany: I realized how ignorant I was.

Perhaps the greatest thing about my 14 years at Tabor Home was Scout Troop 71. It gave me a lifelong love of the outdoors, nature, birds and the environment. Today I strongly oppose the Boy Scout policies against gay troop leaders and its refusal to allow atheists in Scouting. But I cannot repudiate the immense good of Scouting. The joy of camping. The love of an outdoor fire and an indoor fireplace.

Tabor memories, many memories. The Kiwanis and other service club visits and gifts at the holidays. At Christmas the home got an enormous candy cane, at Easter a huge Easter egg. The Pennsylvania state troopers, as I recall, gave each Tabor kid a box of candy at the Yule. And one of the back rooms in the administration building was set aside for a pile of individual presents on Christmas Day.

I recall study hall in the administration building. How we disliked it. Yet it was marvelous discipline. I suspect Tabor kids were better students, because we were forced to study. Still, I hated it when I could not listen to Sunday night radio programs. Going to high school Monday mornings, I heard the town kids relating the jokes on "Amos and Andy" and the Jack Benny program. I felt so deprived. But we Tabor kids did listen to other popular radio programs: "The Shadow Knows," with the devilish laughter of Orson Welles, I think, and "I Love a Mystery" with, I think, Jack, Doc and Reggie.

My favorite teacher at Doylestown High was Jane Kohler. Her teaching of English and journalism inspired me to write and encouraged my love of literature. Allen George was a great history teacher, giving me a start on cynicism about U.S. history. Bill Wolfe was a track coach. I remember the time I was crouched at the starting line to begin a quarter-mile time trial. (I do not recall if it was the fairgrounds dirt track or the new high school cinder track.) Anyway, Mr. Wolfe said: "Now Highton, you know your trouble this year. You're not running fast enough." Indeed. Another quote I remember. Frank Trout, tackle on our football team, said to me at football camp: "How time flies!" And yet in those days we often wished our lives away. "I can't wait for this, I can't wait for that." Today? Time is more precious than money.

One other high school teacher we mocked was the art teacher, who had a bad squint and a strange, pinched voice. I can hear her still: "The point of an onlooker's eye is the eye-level line."

My best friends at Doylestown High were Bill Groman and Dick Leatherman. I remember going to Willow Grove amusement park, about 10 miles south of Tabor, with them. And I recall their astonishment that "this little guy" made the football team by tackling some big guys.

Tabor memories: playing strip poker in a tent in the Tabor woods ... Orv Wright driving me to Penn State one time when his car broke down on the Pennsylvania Turnpike. And another time when Orv and I were fighting "over the Crimea" in the back seat of the Tabor bus returning from church. We were ejected in midtown and forced to walk home. ... And how we kids played war games, fighting in the snow, imagining we were Russian soldiers in World War II. I still have a scar on my right hand between my pinkie and big finger where Carl Hoppe stabbed me.

My favorite weapon was a branch of a beech that curved nicely into the shape of a rifle with a bayonet.

Other memories: May Day, wearing white ducks and parading. I think we even ran around a May Pole pulling a ribbon. ... Tabor woods in spring constantly echoing with the calls of the crested flycatcher. Birdman authority Roger Tory Peterson described the call as "a loud, whistled wheeeee." ... Fridays were special. We had Johnny Cake with syrup for dinner. Then we had Friday night movies. Then on Saturday mornings sword-fighting or playing submariners or whatever we saw on the film the night before. ... Sometimes we had dances. I was a wooden dancer then – and still am.

Occasionally a music teacher would come on campus to give instructions in piano or some other musical instrument. I thought piano playing was sissy stuff so I did not take lessons. I always regretted it. Not that I would have ever been a concert pianist but that I could have noodled – and relaxed – at a piano throughout my life.

Finally, these memories of Tabor Home would be incomplete if I did not speak of Harry Burmeister, the Tabor farmer. Old Boog, as we called him, was a short, round-bellied guy who loved to regale we kids with stories. One of his – and my – favorites was the story of a kid named Redmile. When we were taking in hay, Boog would pitch a forkful of hay with the cry: "Where're you at?" In other words, where were you loading on the wagon? Front corner, back corner, side? One day the wagon started with a jerk and tossed Redmile off. When Boog asked, "Where're you at?" Redmile said "here!" – running up from behind the wagon.

When we worked in the fields in the summer time, the girls would bring us liquid refreshment that we called bug juice, because the insects from the field often flew into the big pot they were carrying. We hoed the truck patch and took in hay in early summer, thrashed wheat in the late summer, dug potatoes in the fall and sometimes husked corn so late in the year that snow was on the ground when we brought in the shucks. Thrashing was a particularly dirty job. At the end of the day we would be black as a chimney sweep. And that reminds me. Don Allison, Taborite and Doylestown High classmate, had to milk the cows at the Tabor barn. I was always embarrassed by this because I did not have to milk.

One of my favorite birding memories was being on top of the wagon gathering corn shucks. An inch or two of snow was on the ground so that when a mouse ran among the corn stubble, the grayness of the mouse appeared unusual against the white. As I was saying to Boog, "Hey, look at the mouse," a sparrow hawk swooped down and caught his lunch. Boog had a boy, Danny, who worshipped me. He followed me everywhere. I guess it was because I liked him and paid attention to him. To this day I love kids.

Enough reminiscences. I often complained about Tabor Home in those distant days. But Tabor taught me independence, self-reliance. It taught me to be satisfied with little. The food never had to be fancy. My clothes did not have to be the finest, very expensive. I never needed the latest technological gadgets. We were not pampered, as kids growing up in their own homes sometimes seemed to be. I did not own a bicycle until I was 21. I did not own a car until I was 22. And the fact that we had to work hard on the Tabor farm was a preparation for the reality of life. In short, the Tabor Home legacy has been with me all my life – for good and for bad.

Jake Highton graduated from Doylestown High School in 1949, Penn State in 1953. He teaches journalism today at the University of Nevada, Reno. He had three girls by his first marriage, which ended in divorce, and is now remarried.

POINT - COUNTERPOINT
By Dorothea Maloney Buckner

When I learned about this project to commemorate 100 years of Tabor Home, I felt the book would capture a lot of stories and memories that would otherwise be lost. On the other hand, I was not sure I wanted to share some of my most inner feelings about growing up at Tabor with the general public. In the end, I concluded the reward was worth the risk.

To me, living at Tabor created internal feelings that were often in conflict. There was a sense of camaraderie established among the kids that was stronger than most families experience. If I could have locked the gates and lived my childhood completely on the Tabor grounds, my sensibilities would have been satisfied. Some of my happiest childhood memories consisted of long, late-evening, philosophical discussions with Jake Highton, and time spent with Eddie Merkel, Joe Hoppe, and Orv and Willy Wright. (I am not sure why all my Tabor friends were male; however, that is beyond the scope of this story.) The reality was that we spent a fair amount of time dealing with the outside world and the insecurities it created.

A personal example should make the point. My younger sister Eleanor and I would occasionally visit our mother in Philadelphia on a Saturday or Sunday. We would ride the local bus back to Tabor from Willow Grove. Instead of getting off at the gate, we would choose to spend an additional 10 cents to ride up to Doylestown and back to Tabor to avoid the stares of the bus passengers as the bus pulled away after our stop. We had only 25 cents to spend for the entire week so an expenditure of almost half of our money was a serious matter. Yet we did it to escape the humiliation of being classified as different.

Without getting into the details of why the Maloney sisters were sent to the Home at ages 3 and 2 respectively, let me say that we were much too young to be institutionalized. With a ratio of about 35 children to every deaconess, there was neither enough time nor inclination to be a mother for each child. There was simply no one to kiss bruised knees and make them better, or offer gentle words of reassurance when disappointments occurred. Life in a children's home was an exercise in survival, with your physical needs being met but not coming close to one's psychological needs.

As far back as I can remember I felt a need to protect my sister. It involved taking the blame for some of her intemperate remarks about Tabor to teachers in elementary school that found their way back to Sister Wilma. There were also mundane events that are hardly worth the re-telling. After walking home from school for lunch that consisted of parsnips, among other delicacies, El was informed by Sister Jenny that she would remain at the lunch table until she consumed every last item on her plate. With tears streaming down her face and the probability looming of being late for school, I quickly snatched the offending vegetables (that I hated with a passion) off her plate and devoured them. My love and concern for my sister's welfare were the motivating factors for my sacrifice. I just couldn't let her get into any more trouble.

As I examine my feelings about living at Tabor from age 3 until graduating from high school, there always seems to be a point followed by a counterpoint. I loved the pretty grounds with trees and small buildings to climb and explore. I was a tomboy and loved climbing on the roofs of the various houses. One time I injured my arm while on top of a small structure in the woods. Rather than report it and get into trouble for being on the roof, I suffered in silence for a week. When children caught communicable diseases, they were put in an isolation ward, either on the third floor of the girls' house or on the second floor of the laundry building. The latter location was more of an adventure if you had several other kids with which to share it. On the one hand, someone would bring you meals, and there would be no chores until you recovered. On the other hand, being by yourself in a remote room was terrifying to me as a small child. For years I would never admit to sickness for fear of being sent to the isolation ward.

Not every memory or perception is necessarily true. As kids, it was generally believed that Sister Wilma did not want us to associate with the family who ran a horse farm located adjacent to Tabor, because they were Catholic. (Tabor was run by Lutheran sisters and we were all convinced that Lutheranism was the only "true" religion.) In retrospect, that belief may have been incorrect. But, because my friend Eddie Merkel was horse-crazy, and I hung around him, I spent some time over on the horse farm. After one of the horses had worked out, I was permitted to lead him back into his stall in the barn. This huge show-horse inadvertently stepped on my foot. When I pulled off my saddle shoe to examine the extent of the damage, I was shocked to see five bloody toes. Of course, I could not report it since I would have had to admit where the accident had occurred. So, I self-medicated my foot and limped around for a week.

There seemed to be a lot of time for recreation, and it was great fun playing kick the can, hop scotch, double-Dutch rope jumping and dodge ball. On rainy days we played pickup sticks or jacks. Yet there also was plenty of work to accomplish. It seemed there were an endless variety of tasks such as canning, scrubbing floors, washing windows, working in the truck patch, weeding and cultivating the vegetables. Canning of tomatoes was particularly difficult. My legs often felt so tired that I could barely remain standing after countless hours in the kitchen.

Like so many of my memories of my 16 years at the Home, my relationship with my mother was not clear-cut. She was quite conscientious about visiting her daughters each week, and I was very proud of her because of that. I don't remember any parent that made a greater effort and was more faithful. Because of her private nursing work schedule, she could not conform to the stated visiting hours. Consequently, she would occasionally show up at Sunday school, church, or even in the classroom. These unscheduled visits irritated Sister Wilma, which caused some tension in their relationship, and it certainly didn't help our cause at all. What my mother failed to realize was that her appearance brought unwarranted attention on children that were already sensitive about being different.

In addition, mother's attempts at disciplining us were not easily accepted, in view of her absentee status. Since I almost always followed the rules, I felt little need for additional guidance on living. All these factors contributed to an uneasy truce with my mother while growing up.

The early years at the Home I considered the worst. I suffered in silence with childhood nightmares. The basic diet we were given (mush and molasses bread in particular) resulted in my being hospitalized with boils. For years I was ashamed of the fact that I lived at Tabor, and my humiliation was highlighted when they sent lunches to elementary school and we had to go to the front of the room to accept them. School kids would make fun of our bus and call it the coffee grinder.

Still, there were many pleasant memories. Swimming in the Tabor pool was a sheer summertime delight, even with its slimy bottom and green sides. We could hardly wait for the three-inch water pipe to fill the pool in the spring. As I remember it, it took a full three days, and the first few days of swimming were really cold! Eating a vine-ripened tomato from the truck patch was an experience to die for. It seemed even more enjoyable because snatching them on the sly was against the rules. The rural setting of Tabor on 100-acres of pristine real estate in Bucks County was simply lovely to behold on an autumn evening. I was thrilled when my eighth grade classmates voted me the girl that contributed most to the Class of '47, and I was presented the American Legion medal at graduation.

Some other childhood memories that just spring into my mind:

- Making leaf huts.
- Rolling up leaves in newspaper and trying to smoke it.
- Sledding in the winter.
- Knocking down ice icicles that were up to two feet in length.
- Learning to cook and enjoying it.
- Watching in horror as Albert Good fell out of the cherry tree and subsequently lost his arm.
- Singing hymns and my religious training at Tabor, which played a significant role in my adult life.
- How sad everyone was when Sister Lena got sick and left the Home.

The transformation from elementary school to high school was easier than I expected, even though I struggled academically because of poor reading skills. It helped that the star halfback of the varsity football team asked me out, much to the chagrin of the cheerleaders who all had their eyes on him. (Imagine, the football captain dating a mere freshman.) I was subsequently selected as a member of the varsity cheerleading squad, which was quite a big deal in high school. The fact that I had to bum a ride with friends to get to the games was a complicating factor and another reminder that Tabor kids did not have parents to assist in daily problem-solving.

It has been more than 50 years since I left Tabor Home, and I still can't decide how I feel about my time there. I cannot imagine sending any of my children to a home, yet living there prepared me for life as an employee, a wife, mother and grandmother. I keep remembering the words to a song in the 1970s entitled "The Gambler": "Every hand's a winner and every hand's a loser." It all depends on how you play the hand you've been dealt.

Dotty Maloney came to Tabor Home as a 3-year-old in 1935 with her 2-year-old sister Eleanor. Her husband of 50 years recently died. She is the mother of four and has five grandchildren. She resides in Doylestown.

I WON TABOR'S FIRST COLOR TV
By Sara Duckworth Carlson

The year was 1940, and it was a sad time. A divorce was breaking up the Duckworth family. Neither parent was able to assume the responsibility for the care of the two girls, 7-year-old Sara and 5-year-old Polly. Grandfather Leon Duckworth had done some research and found Tabor Home to be the closest children's home to Norristown, where we were living. It was decided that it would be advantageous for the girls to live at Tabor while things were so unsettled at home.

Arrival & Transition
Polly and I arrived on a lovely, sunny spring day. In short order, the Duckworth sisters took on the "Tabor look." Tabor girls were traditionally dressed in heavily starched dresses, hair cut short with bangs and long-leg snuggy underwear. They had cotton stockings that had to be worn up under those snuggies and inspected to make sure they were correctly in place. Knee-highs were their attire as warm weather approached. Brown oxfords completed our wardrobe. I thought the shoes were so ugly.

Sister Lena Beideck was the Lutheran Deaconess in charge, and she greeted us upon our arrival. I noticed some young children peering out from the second floor of the laundry building. I found out later that it was the isolation ward where sick kids were housed to reduce the spread of infection. There were a few children on the porch by the big bell and some girls jumping rope. They invited us to play, but Polly had not learned how to jump yet. It was a very scary day, and the events seemed overwhelming.

Part of the adjustment to institutional living was learning all the rules. As one can image, managing 80 children requires structure and rules, and self-discipline is mandatory. Ringing of the big bell, located on the porch of the girls' house, managed events for the children. The first ring was an instruction to wash for meals. The second ring indicated it was time to dine. You could hear the bell everywhere on the property and there was no excuse for being late.

Life was quite regimented. There was a time to get up, eat, do chores, go to school, play, and do homework. Stability and love were very important in our young lives.

Nicknames and name-calling were common, and new kids

were easy targets. I was tall and skinny and with a name like Duckworth, it was inevitable that we heard barbs like "Duck legs," "Ducky," "Daddy long legs," and "Not worth a duck." Sometimes I would choose to ignore the comments, and at other times my response would be a punch for the glib-mouthed talker.

Polly and I did not see eye to eye on all subjects and some of our fights were "lulus." Most of the time she would end up crying and the fight would be over. Many times we could not even remember what started the fracas.

Just a few weeks after our arrival, Polly came down with the measles. The normal isolation area in the laundry building was already full or was being scrubbed down, so she was put on the third floor of the girls' house. I was permitted to talk to her from the second-floor hallway but was not to enter her room. After I caught her disease, it was obvious I had not followed the rule to the letter. The downside was Polly had to remain in isolation with me until I was totally cured.

Physical Layout

Tabor Home was located a mile south of Doylestown on Route 611. They owned about 100 acres of farmland, and the main buildings consisted of a huge administrative building that housed the girls, a converted carriage house where the boys lived, and a two-story laundry building with an attached garage. Across the highway was a barn for 10 or so milking cows and a bull as well as storage space for hay and corn. Various farm animals such as pigs, horses and barn cats also took up residence there. A tenant farmer, Harry Burmeister, occupied a large two-story house near the barn.

The administration building was awesome. It was a three-story mansion with a beautifully curved stairway and banister that led up to the girls' rooms on the second floor. Half way up the second floor was a niche where a grandfather clock was set. We were all impressed with the long chains that wound the clock. Under the stairs was a home reference library and committee room. The secretary's office and the kitchen canning room that contained several large copper kettles and two huge gas stoves (for water bathing and preserving our food) completed the main floor. Both boys and girls ate their meals on the first floor dining room. An alcove with a round table was set for the staff. The younger children ate in the sun porch-type room adjacent to the main room. This also doubled as a homework study hall, which was mandatory.

Within the first year, the Tabor board of directors voted to fund a new girls' dormitory. It was called Strecker Hall and I watched it being built. All the girls were very excited. It was beautiful! We could hardly contain ourselves when we finally moved in. Each girl had her own closet and two drawers in a dresser. Wow! We could now take charge of our own clothes. Weekly inspections ensured our clothes were folded properly and that our closets were kept clean and neat. Our bedspreads and curtains matched and were beautiful. We had washable spreads for "everyday" and put on the "good" ones for special events. Each door had a plaque with the name of the donor. Most of the rooms had four beds and special orange crates were used for books or personal possessions. With a pretty cloth or doily, they made very attractive night stands.

The toddlers' room had five cribs, and there was one room that contained only three beds. Sister Emma Holmes had a private room with bath at one end of the long hall, and a private bathroom at the other end joined two counselors' rooms.

Strecker Hall had the largest bathroom I have ever seen in my life. It contained 20 sinks, five bathtubs in individual enclosures, and five showers with curtains for privacy. It also had five toilets with their own stalls. It took five kids to clean them and two more to sweep and mop the floor. The only thing we really minded was that it was infested with cockroaches. They were big and black and would come out at night. They would scurry away as soon as a light was turned on. No one went barefoot to the bathroom at night. Eventually exterminators were called to destroy the ugly little beasts. We were all so relieved!

There was a state-of-the-art kitchen in Strecker Hall. We had a genuine baker's oven with many racks, a commercial dishwasher that was reserved for special occasions and a huge refrigerator (with locks), as well as a dumbwaiter that brought canned food up from the basement pantry. Only food was allowed to be transported on the dumbwaiter, no children! There was also a large double stove, two ovens and a commercial sized mixer and stainless sink and table. We were all very proud of our kitchen.

A root cellar was located in the basement of the laundry building where we stored potatoes, carrots, onions, squash, and apples to use after the growing season was over. It looked like it might have been used as a coal bin in the past, but it was clean and perfect for storage.

Living Conditions

The general public has always been fascinated by life in a children's home. Tabor was often referred to as the "orphanage," which we all resented. We were not orphans! To us, those were fighting words.

One of our first lessons was that cleanliness was next to godliness. The young girls were taken to the bathroom under the kitchen. It contained two tubs, two or three sinks and a couple of toilets. It was there we were bathed, two or three to a tub, and had our hair washed. We were also taught to brush our teeth.

Monday and Tuesday were washdays. We were only allowed two dresses a week. Mrs. Garonski and Miss Bickel were our laundresses. They starched and ironed the dresses. Select girls were responsible for the rest of the laundry. We had one huge commercial washer, a spinner and a dryer. Most of the time we hung sheets, pillowcases and other white things out to dry in the sun. Towels and washcloths went into the dryer. Laundry was a major operation.

For some reason I had an insatiable appetite and quickly learned where the apple, pear and cherry trees were located on the grounds. We weren't permitted to eat green fruit, but I ate some green apples and got caught. A tablespoon of castor oil was administered, but I cleverly pretended to swallow it. One of the Sisters saw me spitting it out and doubled the size of the dose. On another occasion I consumed too many cherries, which caused a bellyache, and I was sent to bed. I ended up spending hours on the toilet as well as throwing up. Of course, I had to clean up my own mess. I learned a good lesson with that incident. When I discovered patches of strawberries, raspberries or blackberries, I would monitor their progress and eat them only after they ripened. I also ate rose petals, sour grass, elephant ears and stems of dandelions. I survived quite nicely, thank you.

At a much later date, I had severe cramps and a doctor was called in for consultation. After examining me, he asked if I had been out with any boys. After a negative reply, he prescribed cold compresses and bed rest. It turned out it was a mild case of appendicitis. Many years later after leaving Tabor, I had my appendix removed and the surgeon commented that it had almost burst.

After being in Tabor about 18 months, World War II started. Although it didn't mean a whole lot to me when it was announced, it affected everyone. Meat, shoes and gas were rationed. We made balls of aluminum foil out of inner wrapping from chewing gum.

I recall Sister Wilma taking six or eight kids up to Buster Brown Shoe Store on Main Street in Doylestown. We always put our feet into their x-ray machine to see if our shoes were wide and long enough to a last a while.

Rubber and steel became scarce, but life continued. I remember the plastic bags of substitute butter (oleo-margarine), which contained a pea-sized bag of yellow coloring that we had to break and knead so that the oleo looked like butter. It might have looked like butter but it tasted awful. To this day I cannot stand the taste of margarine.

In the summer the older girls were pressed into service helping to home-can fruits and vegetables in season. Some we grew and many came from local businessmen and farmers in the area. When wild strawberries were in season, Sister Wilma would often ask us to bring some home so she could make jam. That was a special treat. Once, as a punishment, I was assigned the task of washing all the two-quart canning jars. We used the kitchen in the admin building for canning as all our supplies, jars and cookers were close by. It was a mammoth job and after it was completed, Sister Wilma informed me that we had an unusually high rate of jars sealed and that I would have the honor of washing the canning jars each year. It was often brought to our attention that every task should be done to the best of our ability. I have tried to follow that philosophy to this day.

We canned and preserved a fair amount of food at Tabor under the watchful eye of the staff. Sauerkraut was a case in point. I can still see Jimmy Good being carried out of the boys' dorm with his feet held high (to keep them clean) and placed into a barrel with shredded cabbage and salt. He would stomp his feet in the barrel (for what seemed like forever) until the barrel was full. Months later we could eat the most delicious sauerkraut and pork. It smelled awful but was it good! It is still one of my favorite meals today. In fact, I am grateful and still use the culinary skills gained at Tabor for my family's canning and preservation of vegetables.

Meals & Leisure Time

Breakfast in the winter consisted of a bowl of hot cereal, a mug of milk and three pieces of molasses bread. The molasses was spread for us and, by the time we ate it, it had soaked completely through the bread. It was absolutely delicious. My mouth still salivates thinking about it. Most of us liked the hot oatmeal and cream of wheat, but we thought Wheatena and cornmeal mush were gross. We looked forward to warmer weather so we could switch to cold cereal.

Grace was said before every meal, and evening devotions consisted of a Bible reading and a hymn. We all ate at tables consisting of eight or 10 to a table with one adult included. Our meals were served family-style. Those of us on K.P. always knew what extra food remained in the kitchen. We would take extra large helpings, knowing there was plenty to refill the bowls.

The young girls and boys at Tabor had plenty of free and unstructured playtime. A lovely playhouse, with Dutch doors and windows painted white with green trim, was available to us. We played house and emulated the home life we missed. It even had stairs on the outside going up to a loft. Much later it became a pen for sheep.

Before the advent of television, radio was king. All the kids would sit in the hallway next to the stairs where the radio was located. We listened to programs like Amos and Andy, Inner Sanctum, The Shadow and The Lone Ranger. It was great fun. I was listening to the radio in December 1941 when it was announced that Pearl Harbor had been attacked and we were at war.

A delivery truck from the Bond Baking Company would drop off bread and other baked goods to the Home. A few of us would help the deliveryman by carrying the items into our kitchen pantry. Occasionally, a little goodie would get misplaced into a secret hiding place and be repatriated at a later date.

Our woods contained an open summerhouse, swings, sliding board, see saws and a huge cement-contained reservoir. We used the reservoir as our base for cops and robbers, king of the hill, and cowboys and Indian games. These activities tended to keep us out of mischief with the operative word being "tended." A set of tree stumps became our store. We could find rainwater in tin cans and make mud pies. Someone was always climbing trees, breaking their bones and catching poison ivy. A paste of baking soda and water was used to cool it down and keep the itching to a minimum. Sometimes you had to soak in the tub, as it was easier that way.

Mr. Neidinger, one of the board members, would visit with his Great Danes. He would allow the younger children to ride on their backs. That was really fun! Other free-time games were jacks, card games like Old Maid and Go Fish, coloring in books, paper dolls, Flinch, checkers and Chinese checkers. In inclement weather we played in the attic of Strecker Hall. Using a big dollhouse and playing with small dolls and furniture was a favorite pastime. We also rode tricycles and bicycles.

As a class of children, Tabor kids were quite innovative. We would create a scooter out of an orange crate and some roller skates by mounting the skates on the bottom board of the crate, fix a handle and, voila, a home-made vehicle. Foot-power would propel the scooter and give hours of fun.

Winter was a bit more challenging for leisure time activities because of the cold weather, but ice skating and sledding were two sports that all the kids relished. We went as a group to the "rocks" in Edison located on the Neshaminy Creek. During one ice-skating event as spring was approaching, we could see running water and intellectually knew the ice was not that thick, but the urge to skate overcame common sense and one girl fell through the ice. The water was shallow but she panicked, and it was obvious we had to get her out quickly. I remember getting on my stomach and instructing a boy to pull me backwards after I reached the victim. We worked together and pulled her out. We quickly built a bon fire, removed her wet clothes and wrapped her in a blanket. After she and her clothes were dry, we returned home. The only injury was my scraped knee.

Sledding was usually done on the lawns or the wagon path (long curving drive-way that led from the main gate to the admin building). But sometimes we would sled in the meadow located by the farmer's house across Route 611. It was a long hill, sloping and twisting and terminating at the creek. Inevitably, someone ended up in the water and his or her sledding was finished for the day. Polly and I received a Mickey Mouse sled one Christmas with our names burned in on the bottom. That was proof-positive that it was our sled when other kids were using it. Our sled was still working in 1951 when I left Tabor and I took it with me. I still have scars from aggressive sled riders running over my hands. We were a tough group of kids.

School

By the time the Duckworths arrived, Tabor had stopped home schooling at the cottage on the grounds. Grades one through eight attended Edison School and nine through 12 went to Doylestown High School. Pop Schaeffer was principal at Edison, but Paul Kutz replaced him in 1941. Paul and his wife Martha taught seventh and eighth grades. In the same time frame, Sister Lena retired and was replaced by Sister Wilma Loehrig as head deaconess.

In nice weather we Taborites walked to school in double lines and rode the Tabor bus if the weather was bad. The bus was blue and white, and I do not remember any bars on the windows.

School lunch consisted of two sandwiches, one bologna with mustard and one peanut butter and jelly. We would get a piece of fruit if it were available. The girls on kitchen duty usually made all the sandwiches. We worked a week at a time in the kitchen.

In third grade I recall other students leaving their pencils on their desks. I just picked them up and deposited them in my desk. After several kids complained about their missing pencils, a desk check was conducted and I made my first visit to the principal's office. I think I received a whipping. Sometimes punishment consisted of sitting on a stool or writing sentences many times until the teacher thought the lesson was learned.

I loved writing poems, singing and art. I was soon inducted into chorus. Spelling came quite easy for me. Math, which included fractions, was my least favorite subject.

All students had their hearing checked every other year. It was soon apparent I wasn't hearing very well, and in the summer of 1946 I received my first hearing aid. Very few hearing aids were worn at that time, and I was very sensitive about having one. Kids would tease me, and I became somewhat withdrawn.

During my eighth grade year, "Tom Sawyer" was an operetta presented by the elementary school, and I portrayed Aunt Polly. I remember singing a solo, and it was very exciting.

In ninth grade, ugly white gym suits were mandatory, and the batteries for my hearing aid hung out below my suit. I was totally embarrassed, but I learned to live with it. In health class, I presented a report to the class on nerve deafness and the inner-workings of a hearing aid. I had graphs and charts to aid me, and the teacher awarded me an "A." Life became a little easier for me.

I progressed at a normal rate through high school and received average to above-average grades, but I never really considered any post-high school education. When I graduated in 1950, I received a check for $100 from Dr. McKinney, President of the Tabor board of directors. I was the only Tabor graduate that year. Sister Wilma took me to Philadelphia and helped me pick out a typewriter with my windfall. Again, I felt quite special and loved. When learning to drive, Sister Wilma gave me several driving lessons too.

Special Days

If you ever attend a gathering of Tabor alumni, the subject will eventually get around to special days. They all seem to have fond remembrances of Christmas or May Day or Easter or their birthday. Tabor always made a big deal out of special days.

Christmas was the most special day in the eyes of many of the children. It seemed we celebrated it most of December. Our Tabor family was invited to several nearby churches. Burholme (near Philadelphia) and Lansdale are the two I remember. We shared their church service, were invited into their homes for dinner and went back to church and received gifts. We presented a skit or sang songs. It was wonderful!

The owner of the Bucks County Playhouse treated us to many enjoyable, free movies. We were also given a box of hardtack candy, nuts, and an apple and orange. Sometimes I found a few pieces of fruit thrown out on the street. I would pick them up and take them home, because I felt it was disrespectful to throw food away. Even today I feel thankful for the kind and generous heart of the owner of the theater.

Policemen, firemen, businessmen, and many church and women's groups volunteered their time. A local high school student, Wilma Kummer, would serenade us on her accordion. It seemed like the entire community would turn out to make Christmas special for Tabor kids.

May Day was an open house and fundraiser for the Home each year. The kids worked for weeks getting everything cleaned up and ready; getting out the good spreads, polishing the floors and washing up the good dishes that were stored in the closet behind the boys' dorm. Vendors came and set up booths to sell their wares. If our parents came it was extra fun, as we would have some money to spend. It wasn't such a great time for kids without visitors or money. One downside to the day was that we ate lunch over in the laundry room on makeshift tables, a huge step down from eating in Strecker Hall.

One booth that was everyone's favorite was one that sold baked goods like cakes, homemade cookies and candy. Another had a lemon on a candy stick. It was cheap and lasted a long time. Tabor kids had a booth, and all year we worked at sewing, embroidering and making things to sell.

After lunch, around two o'clock, it was show time. We would all assemble in the auditorium to put on our costumes and practice our lines. I recall one year we had crepe paper costumes and were a country garden full of flowers and butterflies. Once the auditorium started filling up, it was time for silence. Only whispering was allowed and no flushing of toilets backstage. Finally, the curtain lifted. Lights, camera, action! Much to my dismay, I had to go to the bathroom and could not hold it. As other actors mouthed their lines, I stood quietly by and let it trickle down my leg, into my shoe and onto the floor. I just continued as if nothing had happened, but it was one of the most embarrassing episodes in my limited show business career.

Memorial Day was great for several reasons. It marked the end of the school year, and it meant swimming season, everyone's favorite, was upon us. It was also a time for vacationing with our parents. Sister Wilma had me take a Red Cross and Life Saving Course, which I completed. That allowed me to assist at our pool when Life Guards were not available.

Even though we all loved our pool, it was not state-of-the-art. It did not have proper filters, nor were chemicals used to keep it clear. After a month or so, the water would turn green and slime would accumulate on the bottom and sides. At that point, the pool would be drained, the algae would be scrubbed away and fresh water would be used to refill the pool. The one-inch pipe available was quite slow. It would take almost three days for the water to refill. It was quite frustrating to us to watch the whole process, which seemed to go in slow motion.

Another special day was going to Atlantic City as guests of one of the Tabor board members, Mr. Neidinger. It was quite a treat. Some of us would go down a day early and help open the house and prepare the facilities for the other Tabor kids. We would make up beds and help prepare the food. We felt so grown up. We all swam in the Atlantic Ocean, sat on the beach and walked around on the boardwalk. A highlight was attending the stage show on Steel Pier. I still remember seeing the horse jumping off the ramp into a pool with a rider on its back. I was so inspired that I told Sister Wilma I wanted to be on the stage someday.

At Easter, the Palace of Sweets, a candy store on State Street in Doylestown, would make and display a huge, decorated, chocolate covered egg. They gave this monstrous treat to Tabor Home each year. It would be cut up and divided among all the children. We thought it was absolutely the best Easter candy we ever ate.

Birthdays were our last special day. We all loved them. A homemade cake was baked, the birthday boy or girl was sung to, and it made the recipient feel extra special. Each table in Strecker Hall received a birthday cake, and with 80 birthdays a year there was a lot of cake consumed.

Successes & Failures

It is a little peculiar to categorize your childhood with successes and failures, but with 40 "brothers" and 40 "sisters" a competitive spirit was a necessity. My most obvious success occurred after Sister Wilma informed me that a local business was having a contest. It was a poetry competition with the winning entry being awarded a Crosley Color Console Television. One must remember that this was before individual houses owned color TV sets. She handed me the entry form and said the rest was up to me. I completed the poem and submitted it the next day. It turned out that my entry took first place, and Tabor ended up with a beautiful color set. I was so proud to win that prize. For some reason, not too many kids were aware how we actually obtained the set. It was set up in the admin building and afforded a lot of kids many hours of entertainment.

Several other successes have already been documented like my rescue of the girl that fell through the ice, my graduating from high school, on-stage performances and my report on hearing aids. I know these are not events that are world changing, but to a Tabor kid even a little success was a big happening.

Failures may be too strong a word for the following incidents. Perhaps bad luck or poor planning might be more appropriate. The first was a caper involving four girls: Catherine Kniese, my sister Polly and me, and Catherine Mott (I could be mistaken about her). Our plan was to highjack some molasses from the cellar in the admin building, where a 55-gallon barrel was located. We filled our two-quart jar full and headed for the lawn under a huge evergreen pine tree to consume our wanton goodies, feeling very smug that we had pulled it off. Somehow, Sister Wilma found out and meted out severe punishment: Eat only molasses bread for each meal until the two-quart jar was empty. We lost the battle but won the war. We were all ecstatic with the harsh sentence. It was our very favorite food!

The first two years, Polly and I lived on the third floor of the girls' dorm. We had a chamber pot in the hallway for emergencies. One night I got my sister up to use the pot, but she got stuck when she was finished. After pondering the problem, I figured out how to release the vacuum and separate Polly from her horrible dilemma. I was greatly relieved.

Emptying the chamber pot was assigned to the older girls. I distinctly remember Shirley Allison was carrying the hazardous cargo down the stairs to dispose of it when she stumbled and the waste flew all over the stairs and onto the beautifully carved stairway. What a mess! All available hands scurried to clean it up. You just don't forget a failure like that.

Post-Tabor

I stayed on after graduation and worked in the boys' dorm and grew up rather quickly. Being responsible for ensuring that 25 boys got their showers and were clean behind the ears was interesting, to say the least. I always felt working with boys was much easier than working with girls. There were no hidden agendas. What you see is what you get. Girls were moody and easily provoked. I received $80 a month plus room and board for full-time employment. At the time I felt quite wealthy.

The same year I became engaged to a high school classmate, Jim Carlson, and Pastor Repass married us in February of 1952.

Reflections

I feel my life has been blessed with a caring husband and loving family. I often pray to the Lord as I work around my home.

I thank him for the many wonderful blessings he has bestowed upon me. I thank Tabor Home for the many lessons in living I have learned and especially to Sister Wilma for being my surrogate mother.

Sara Duckworth came to Tabor Home with her younger sister Polly in the spring of 1940 and remained there for 11 years. She is the mother of three girls and lives in White Cloud, Mich. Her husband died several years ago just shy of 52 years of marriage.

GOD BLESS THE STAFF AT TABOR HOME
By Polly Duckworth Harris

My parents separated in 1940, and, with neither spouse capable of supporting my sister Sara and me, we were shipped off to Tabor Home from Norristown, where we were living. I was 5 years old and the younger of the Duckworth sisters.

Despite having my sister around for moral support, the uprooting from a family environment to a children's home was traumatic for me. I was afraid of everything, and it took me a long time to adjust to the new regimen. I was separated from Sara and put in the "babies' room" with four other preschool age children. To make matters worse, I caught the measles during the first month and was put into an isolated room on the third floor of the girl's house. To be confined by yourself in an "attic jail" is the worst nightmare for a 5-year-old.

Although the staff of women deaconesses were dedicated and concerned about the welfare of each child, they were not trained in the psychology of children separated from their parents at an early age. Bedwetting was a common disorder at Tabor, and it was addressed by attempting to humiliate the offender. He or she was required to wash and hang their soiled sheets on the line for all the other children to see. In severe cases, the child was forced to sleep in the bathtub until the appalling behavior ceased. Of course, the solution was quite inappropriate.

It was always upsetting to me when people referred to Tabor as the orphanage, as that implied I had no living parents. But, in fact, there were a lot of similarities. Sunday was visiting day, and we would all anticipate the arrival of a joyous visit from a father or mother. Most of the time we would end the day with disappointment. My mother would come two or three times a year. My father started out visiting twice a month. But, after his second marriage, he seldom showed up. If there was one lesson that I learned in my 12 years at the Home, it was never get a divorce and be placed in a position that you would have to put your children in an institution.

Even though it was a hard knock life, there were a lot of happy times. I loved the daily swimming in our pool, the yearly trip to Atlantic City in the summer and building soapbox derby vehicles from orange crates and roller skate wheels. There were cherry and apple trees to climb, fruit to pick over at Farm School for some spending money (some of us ate more than we picked), as well as Sunday school and church for spiritual reinforcement.

Kid-power was a valuable resource at Tabor, and it was harnessed to run the farm and keep the Home looking spick and span. That meant kitchen chores, weeding the vegetables in the truck patch, sweeping all the pavements and the wagon path leading down to the main gate, and mowing the acres of grass surrounding the buildings. The boys did most of the outside chores with the girls relegated to inside work. I can't tell you how many pots and pans I cleaned and scoured while growing up.

I have mixed feelings about school. We all attended Doylestown Township Consolidated School for grades one through eight. It was located in Edison, a small town about a half-mile south of Tabor. We would walk to school in single file down Route 611 under the watchful eye of the school patrol, whose badges and white sashes signified their authority. I sometimes felt we were in a chain gang.

I was always an average student and earned average grades. I probably didn't put enough value in striving for A's. Part of the problem was the fact that Tabor kids all felt like second-class citizens, because we were from the Home. The "normal" students looked down on us, as you might view a group of homeless people lining up for soup. It was always uncomfortable. The teachers were, by and large, understanding and helpful.

I was not a model student, but I seldom got in trouble. I did get into a hair-pulling fight with Eleanor Maloney (a friend from Tabor) for some obscure reason and was punished by both the school and Sister Wilma. On another occasion I sneaked out of my room at night to see a boyfriend and ran into one of the summer counselors meeting with her boyfriend at the same spot. She obviously did not report me. Did I mention the times several of us paid nightly visits to the committee room through an unlocked window to borrow some of the candy supplies that were stashed there for future use? Or the molasses stored in barrels that we sampled between meals? When I say I seldom got into trouble, what I really mean is, I didn't often get caught carrying out my indiscretions.

One unusual habit that I had was catching small toads in the sandbox over by the swimming pool and keeping them in my clothes drawer for safekeeping. Of course, I would forget that I had stored them there and several days later I would have to dispose of the corpses.

With the hindsight of 60 years and the experience of 53 years as a mother and wife, I believe I absorbed many valuable lessons from years at Tabor.

- Respecting other people's property as well and learning how to relate to others.
- The importance of reinforcing good behavior and discouraging bad behavior. I am not implying that any or all methods used at Tabor were effective.

I have an immense appreciation for the people responsible for running the Home. They had a vision to see the need to provide for children from broken homes and give them a stable and secure environment. They were not perfect, but they did the best they could under very trying circumstances. God Bless the staff at Tabor Home for their efforts, sacrifice and successes.

Polly Duckworth and her older sister Sara came to Tabor Home in 1940 and remained there for 12 years. She is the mother of seven children and resides in Pennsburg, Pa., with her husband of 53 years, Richard.

MY UPBRINGING WAS WONDERFUL
By Emily Mumaw Brunk

My mother died when I was almost 3 years old, and my father was left with nine children to raise. By the time I was 5, it was evident that the financial, emotional and time demands of child-rearing were overwhelming for him. I ended up in Tabor Home in 1939. Two older sisters, Doris and Kathleen, followed several years later but stayed for a shorter period.

Unlike many young children who are traumatized by family separation, I actually liked the idea of getting to live in such a large, warm house where all the girls lived. Looking back, I don't remember having any period of adjustment. It just felt normal from the first day at Tabor. It is possible that a child from such a large family may not notice much difference between nine siblings at home and 40 girls at Tabor that seemed like sisters.

Some of my memories of those 13 years are quite vivid, such as being taken to the shoe store in Doylestown, 20 children at a time, and being asked only if the shoes fit. If the answer was yes, you had a new pair of shoes. Contrast that with taking a teenage girl for shoes today. The image is striking. Or lining up for toothpaste for tooth-brushing morning and evening. And the dreaded dose of castor oil that came on Sunday nights. I don't know a single soul that did not hate that! No one ever questioned any of the procedures that were carried out at the Home. You did what you were told, and that was that.

I don't mean to imply that we were robots that never had a single innovative thought. I remember confiscating raw potatoes and eating them. And my favorite story was the time a group of boys and girls decided to ride the dumb-waiter down to the storeroom on the bottom floor of the new girls' house. Two of the smaller girls got into the cramped enclosure and we were lowered on pulleys the 12 or 15 feet into the locked vault where food was stored. We carried enough bread and molasses back up the dumbwaiter for a royal feast, and distributed it to the adventurous band of kids who had planned the attack. One of the girls confessed to Sister Wilma, and the entire band of marauders was sentenced to stand on the stage during evening meal for a week, with our only sustenance being bread and molasses sandwiches. Tabor kids were fairly accustomed to public humiliation, so I'm not sure if the punishment was too effective.

Another memory etched on my mind was the ringing of the dinner bell on Sunday morning as a reminder to get on the Tabor bus, and lining up and receiving a penny for Sunday school offering and a penny for church. St. Paul's Lutheran Church did not get rich from the Tabor kids in attendance.

When I left Tabor I got a job as a telephone operator, followed by several accounting jobs. I even sold Anheiser beer for a while. I married in 1958, had two wonderful children and have no regrets about my life. I tell everyone I had a wonderful upbringing at Tabor Home, never got spanked and learned many homemaking skills, which came in handy later in life. I often wish my grandchildren would live as disciplined a life as I did.

Emily Mumaw was 5 years old when she came to Tabor Home in 1939. She remained there until she was 18. Two of her sisters, Doris and Kathleen, were also in the Home for several years. She is living in Indianapolis, Ind., near her daughter.

VISITING JOE HOPPE
By Orville Wright

Joe Hoppe's health had been declining for the past eight years. He had been diagnosed with prostate cancer in 1994 during a routine physical examination and was undergoing chemotherapy treatments to counter the disease. The side effects of the remedy as well as the prescribed drugs were having a telling effect on his normally positive outlook on life. Several telephone conversations with him indicated his morale was not approaching world class.

Joe was a Tabor alumnus, having reported to the Home in 1937 at the age of 4, along with his younger brother Carl. A third Hoppe (Bobby), barely 2 years old, would follow a year later. Joe left high school before graduating and spent a 20-year military career in the Army and Air Force as a jet engine mechanic. His last duty station was Altus Air Force Base in Altus, Okla., located in the southwest corner of the state.

Two of Joe's childhood friends, Don Fritz and Dotty (Dorothea Maloney) Buckner, were living in the greater Doylestown area and several times expressed concern about Joe's mental and physical health. Don had arrived at Tabor with his older sister Billie Jane in 1945 at age 11. Dotty was a 10-year veteran of the Home by that time, having entered at age 3 along with her 2-year-old sister Eleanor. Both Don and Dotty graduated from Central Bucks High School and were popular members of their class, Don as an accomplished athlete and Dotty as a varsity cheerleader.

Don's wife Martha suggested taking action and paying Joe a visit. With the idea proposed, the planning started to take shape. In the end, the trio of Don, Dotty and me met in the Philadelphia airport and flew to Dallas on the 17th of January 2003. We rented a large auto (as the days of slim athletes were long gone) and drove the 200 miles to Altus.

I had previously purchased a portable tape recorder to use in editing the Book of Memories to celebrate the 100th anniversary of Tabor Home in 2007. Armed with the recorder, a cellular phone and 50-year-old stories, we plopped down in row 21 on U.S. Air Flight 1589 bound for reminiscence lane. Keep in mind that none of us had seen Joe in 20 or 25 years and age has a funny way of disguising one's appearance. Hair tends to thin or disappear, and modern clothes dryers are designed to shrink trousers such that a

34-inch waist measurement is only a fond recall. Don took the aisle seat and immediately commented on how much narrower the airlines were making their seats these days.

The three-hour flight to Texas consisted of "sea stories" about Tabor in the 1940s and early '50s, interrupted only by the flight attendant offering a small bag of pretzels and a soft drink over the lunch hour. Locating an appropriate restaurant as soon as we cleared the Dallas-Fort Worth metropolitan area became a priority.

Recovering our bags and obtaining our rental car went surprisingly smooth. We managed the complex labyrinth of highways surrounding Dallas and Fort Worth and were heading northeast toward the Red River in no time. Unfortunately, as we left the civilized urban sprawl of the Big D, acceptable eating establishments also disappeared. It was another hour before we spotted any restaurants. The place we selected by default featured giant hamburgers and burritos. Men in cowboy hats and families out of one of John Steinbeck's novels had also chosen our survival location. We ordered their Texas-sized specialty, paid the $13 bill for all three lunches, and resumed our quest. I received a verbal lashing from my ungrateful companions for recommending we clear the suburbs before dining.

Oklahoma is not the prettiest state in the union, and its stark landscape was something of a disappointment to residents of Bucks County, as we crossed the Red River. Altus is a typical blue-collar Oklahoma city in the Great Plains country. It has a population of 23,000 residents and has a history dating back to 1886. A flood destroyed the entire town in 1891 so the survivors chose to relocate the residential area two miles east, out of the flood plain. Its economy is dependant upon the local Air Force Base, and Altus is known locally for its Rock-N-Rumble car show, the Cotton Pickin' Chili Cook-off and the Candy Cane Cash $10,000 giveaway. Of the three major motels in town, we selected the $50-a-night Ramada Inn, located in the heart of the action, in conformance with our group persona.

After check-in we contacted Joe, who immediately drove the two miles from his house to greet his childhood friends from Pennsylvania. We decided to spend the first evening meal together at the only Chinese Restaurant in town. It was a buffet-type arrangement, and Tabor stories dominated the meal. In no time we were all back at Tabor and stories and memories like these just seemed to come to life over dinner:

- One warm evening, three or four of us decided to sneak into the girls' house and visit one of the rooms. It was probably Eddie Knauss' idea, but Joe Hoppe and Don Fritz were participants. We shimmied up the girls' laundry chute and met in Patsy Oxinio's room. (There were always four girls per room.) One of the boys whispered "chicky" (code word for someone's coming), and the boys dived under one of the beds. When it appeared that it was a false alarm, they all came out and were socializing when a summer counselor appeared at Patsy's door, squinting. Her coke-like glasses were missing from her face, so it was obvious her visual acuity was somewhat impaired. "I know you're in here, whoever you are," she offered, followed by, "I know who you are, so leave now." The raiders brazenly departed via the front steps. However, the following day, several of the guilty parties plus at least one innocent member were called into Sister Wilma's office and were sentenced to one week on the stage with no dinner plus weeding of the truck patch by hand. (The latter task was equivalent to at least several of the 12 labors of Hercules.) Don, assigned to the barn for daily duties, told Harry Burmeister, the Tabor farmer, of his plight, and Harry obliged by cultivating the field the first day Sister Wilma took some time off and was absent from the grounds.
- There were many cases of older children taking advantage of younger ones. We all considered it a rite of passage to take advantage of ignorance. Joe found some droppings in his rabbit pen and carefully collected them in his hand. He spotted a new kid, Tucker Price, and as an act of kindness offered the "chocolate raisins" to him. It did not take long for Tucker, after chewing the gift, to realize the candy offering was anything but. Joe found the event hilarious.
- Most of the boys turned into iconoclasts (believers that nothing is sacred) in short order. Nothing was too cruel to say to another child. Thin skin thickened up in a hurry in that environment. Freddy Disque had lost a front tooth, and the other teeth had pushed the remaining front tooth to the middle of his mouth. Carl Hoppe observed to Freddy that it would be very funny if he, Freddy, lost all the rest of his teeth except the lone front tooth in the middle of his mouth. Freddy failed to see the humor in the cruel observation.

- Joe Hoppe was eating his evening meal at Sister Wilma's table, and she observed that he had consumed a complete loaf of bread. His punishment was to stand on the stage overlooking the dining room (public humiliation was an accepted means of discipline) and continuously repeat, "I am a pig. I am a pig. I am a pig."

- Occasionally a crime was too serious for a sentence of missed meals or extra chores. Lynford Disque (Freddy's youngest brother) once buried a chicken alive in the back yard. He spent a great deal of time on the stage while we ate our meals, and when everyone received a Christmas stocking, Limpy's was full of coal, the absolute in punishment.

- Sister Wilma personally owned several collie dogs during her tenure as the head administrator at Tabor Home. A number of the boys would mistreat her dog when she was not present. It was little wonder that the dogs became somewhat aggressive around young boys. Don Fritz was running around the old girls' house (present-day administration building) when her dog nipped at his heels. He stopped and gave the dog a kick, not knowing that Sister Wilma observed the episode from her window. She opened the window and remarked, "Hello, Mr. Bully."

- Sitting around a radio in the evening listening to The Lone Ranger, The Shadow (The weed of crime bears bitter fruit. Who knows what evil lurks in the hearts of men? The Shadow knows!), Gang Busters, Inner Sanctum, Amos and Andy, and Jack Armstrong, the All American Boy.

- Eating mulberries and cherries from the numerous fruit trees on the property. Picking strawberries at Farm School for 2 or 3 cents a quart. Listening to the results of the day's picking and the big disparity between the serious pickers and those who came over just to eat their fill of strawberries. (Don Fritz was banned from future picking when his total output was announced as one quart of berries from a full day of labor.)

The first evening in Altus concluded with a plan to meet Joe after breakfast and spend the morning at his house, meeting his wife Sam and looking at old pictures. A visit to the base was on the schedule as well as a quick stop at his burial stone.

Joe met us at the appointed hour after a forgettable complimentary breakfast at the hotel. We were welcomed at his house by his dog Macho, who indicated by his hostile demeanor that he wanted nothing to do with visitors from back East. The Tabor stories continued interspersed with Joe and Sam reviewing their early days of courtship in Southeast Asia. Sam was born and raised in Thailand and has been reluctant to abandon her native culture completely in adjusting to life in the United States. She loves her large screen television set that has one Thai channel. Their two children live within commuting distance of Altus, and they visit periodically.

The afternoon was spent touring the Air Force base where Joe had spent more than 20 years as a civil servant jet engine mechanic. We then drove by the cemetery where Joe and Sam will be interred eventually. Their tombstone was impressive, but seeing one's name on a monument is a bit daunting, as if you are looking into the future.

Our last evening in Altus was spent dining in an upscale steak and fish house. The special was an all-you-can-eat buffet for $10. The tone was lighthearted with a plentiful supply of stories, laughter and nostalgia. It was as though we realized how lucky we were to have survived the random nature of life and could all be together in an obscure town in Oklahoma eating dinner and reminiscing about the "good old days" of our youth. It was a much simpler time in which we took happiness and future success for granted. Life was about laughter, loyalty, friendship and an unspoken love for all Tabor kids who had fought the good fight! Some other stories:

- When Dotty Maloney was a freshman at Doylestown High, she started dating the star halfback on the varsity football team, Bruce Tenley. It was certainly enough to make any young girl's head swim, but particularly a Tabor girl. Needless to say, the established clique of the high school in-crowd was less than pleased to lose this most dateable catch to a freshman. With Sister Wilma's blessing and a midnight curfew, Bruce took Dotty out on a Saturday evening date. As the bewitching hour came and passed, Sister Wilma picked up the phone and called the Tenley house inquiring about the whereabouts of young Dorothea. Bruce's parents were less than thrilled to be awakened at 12:30 a.m., and the participants learned a hard lesson as the relationship terminated involuntarily.

- Remember how Jake (Highton) used to learn a new vocabulary word every day? Don Fritz recalled that Jake used to open his window for fresh air even on the coldest of nights. Don threatened to nail Jake's window shut one of these winter nights. In fact, he just locked the window and waited for Jake's reaction. As Jake attempted to open the window with no success, he shouted, "You dirty rat, Fritz. You did nail my window shut, didn't you?"

- Speaking of harsh punishments at the Home, one of the worst was the silent treatment handed out by Sister Wilma for various indiscretions. Because she controlled virtually every extracurricular event off the grounds, if she wasn't speaking to you, you were essentially grounded. That included sports, movies, fishing, going to town or visiting friends. It was the most effective punishment.

- A farm is not inherently a safe environment, especially for youngsters. Whether it is driving a tractor, putting hay in the loft or dealing with farm animals, there is potential for injury. One of the Guernsey milking cows had just given birth, and Don (Fats) Allison had taken the calf to a nearby stall. The mother was released from her neck stanchion and immediately charged toward Fats and gored him in the groin area, tearing his trousers. Fortunately, her horn missed all vital organs, and Don escaped unharmed, but thoroughly shaken.

- A favorite memory for many Tabor kids in the late '30s and mid-'40s was the annual trip to Atlantic City. The Tabor bus would transport a number of the children to the New Jersey resort town as the guests of Mr. Neidinger, a member of the Tabor Home board of directors. They would swim in the Atlantic Ocean or sun on the beach or walk on the fabled boardwalk. Admission to Steel Pier was included in the outing as well as a meal. It was not uncommon for the whole bus to sing songs on the trip down and back. Life was good! Dotty Buckner recalled sitting in the stands at Steel Pier when a nice-looking teenage boy passed a note to her, requesting a meeting. As she introduced herself to the self-styled Lothario, the next words out of her mouth were that she was just visiting a friend and was not from Tabor. Maybe life wasn't that good.

- Food played a big role in every kid's life, and it was especially meaningful at Tabor. For five years in the early '40s, food was rationed and ration stamps were used to procure many foods that were in short supply. Looking back, molasses bread was a staple and was such a favorite that it was used as a means of exchange. Kids would trade or bet molasses bread instead of real money. Other examples: red beet gelatin (awful!); red beets, rice and stew (commonly referred to as a typical Tabor meal); Mrs. Shaw's tomato gravy over macaroni (heavenly!); sauerkraut over mashed potatoes (sounds terrible but was pretty good); rolled lamb or veal (good and it made great gravy); oven-browned potatoes (wonderful); bug juice (Kool aid that was brought out to the hay fields on hot summer days); Thanksgiving, Easter and Christmas dinners (everyone's favorite meals).

After a final breakfast at Denny's, we headed south to the Dallas airport. We planned to watch the Philadelphia Eagles crush the Tampa Bay Bucs in 15-degree weather at Vet Stadium. Unbeknownst to us, our hotel changed its name, and it took us 60 minutes to find our temporary home even though we knew it was located "one mile north of the airport." We finally arrived just in time to see the kickoff and the Eagles score in the first minute of the game. Little did we know what was in store for the mighty Philadelphia team.

Our last meal together was long and delightful. It was as if we sensed that this adventure was almost over and wanted to savor the joy associated with it. There was also a bit of sadness with the realization that we might never see Joe again.

The flight from Dallas left on time, and the three hours passed quickly. Bags were recovered, and Don's wife met the Bucks County travelers for the final 30-mile leg of the odyssey.

As a postscript, Joe called Dotty the next day and stated how grateful he was for the visit and reported that our visit had "put the zip back in my life."

Joe Hoppe started at Tabor in 1937 at the age of 4. The last stop of his 20-year military career was at Altus Air Force Base in Altus, Okla., the town where Joe retired with his wife Sam.

I NEVER DEVELOPED INTELLECTUAL CURIOSITY
By Orville Wright

Most people envision that children's homes or orphanages are quite similar to the one to which Dickens' Oliver Twist was condemned. Or, perhaps like the one housing Little Orphan Annie or Father Flanagan's Boy's Town in Nebraska. In truth, there are probably as wide a variation among institutions housing children as there are among two-parent households in the country. Any generalization such as "foster homes are good, institutions are bad" is as wrong as often as it is right.

It is fair to say that any child institutionalized at a young age will end up with a set of values and a personality different than if he had been raised by a set of loving and supportive parents. But, as far as a predictor for success in life, one could make a convincing argument favoring the parentless child.

Tabor Home for Children was located one mile south of Doylestown. The physical layout of the Home was impressive. The starting point was the massive 18-foot high black gate with the words TABOR HOME FOR CHILDREN adorned in gold paint across the top. A winding road surrounded by green lawns and trees ended in a circular drive at the administrative building, originally a mansion built for Philip A. Fretz. On the right side of the road a softball field was situated with a homemade backstop, constructed of chicken wire, that kept passed balls from rolling into the woods. There was a swimming pool that was used during the summer months. Every 45 days the algae would coat the sides with a green slime. The pool would then be emptied and the sides cleaned. The two and one-half-inch water pipe would deliver clean swimming water for another month and a half. Watching the pool refill seemed to take an eternity. In fact, it took almost three days. The water was frigid when the pool reopened, but the sun and children's body heat soon rectified that.

The rest of the acreage consisted of agricultural fields that produced potatoes, hay, wheat and corn. In addition, there was a "truck patch" that was located adjacent to the main gate, right on Route 611. A variety of vegetables were grown and cultivated in this humongous garden. Tabor kids all developed skills in weeding that would benefit them throughout their lifetime. Across the highway were the barn, additional fields and the tenant farmer's house. The remainder of the land was covered with wooded terrain, which the boys utilized as a huge battleground. The country was at war, and simulated combat was a favorite pastime for the youngsters living there.

The staff consisted of five full-time Lutheran sisters augmented by several part-time assistants in the summer months when all 80 children were not in school. The children attended Doylestown Township Consolidated School, a half mile down the road in Edison, Pa. Following graduation from the eighth grade, students enrolled in Doylestown High School. The Home did not have a good high school graduation record in the late 1930s, particularly among the girls. Sometimes a 16-year-old girl was requested to pack up and leave following minor violations of house rules, such as sassing a Sister.

Arriving at Tabor in September of 1941 was traumatic for both my brother Will (age 6) and me (age 7). But children are quite adaptable. They accept situations over which they have minimal say. The girls' house, in the final stages of completion, was an impressive two-story stone dormitory that housed 40 girls from age 5 to 17. It contained a huge dining room, a restaurant-sized kitchen and locked storerooms packed with canned fruits, vegetables and juices. These rooms were targeted by bands of hungry boys intent on appropriating number 10 cans of fruit, such as peaches, pears or apricots. It also housed an auditorium in the basement, which was used for meetings, religious services and to stage plays and musicals. On the second floor were about 12 rooms, each accommodating four girls to a room. The second floor was off limits to boys. But sometimes boys would sneak to the girls' rooms at night.

The boys' house was a cut granite structure, converted in 1922 from an old carriage house and consisting of two large dormitory-style bedrooms on the second floor. The front room housed the younger children up to age 12 or 13. The back room was where the big guys lived. Each child in the front room owned a 12-inch by 12-inch cubbyhole where his clothes were stored, plus a hook to hang up the wardrobe. It was similar to a "one on, one off and one in the wash" scenario.

Boys also stored their baseball gloves, bats, balls and other sports gear in a seat-type chest on the ground floor. Laundry was done on Mondays and kids were responsible for getting their dirty clothes in the laundry bag by Sunday night.

Every child was assigned a number, which was stitched on each piece of clothing to show ownership. My number was 111. I was quite proud of it. Owning anything was not important to Tabor kids, commonly swapping clothes and sporting equipment. The ground floor contained a glassed-in rectangular porch, where all the lock boxes were located. A large playroom with hardwood floors was also located on the same floor, and one passed through a smaller playroom en route to the downstairs boys' bathroom. The bathroom consisted of about four stalls for toilets in a big shower room. A weekly shower was prescribed, but no one was fanatic about enforcing it. The third floor was unused during normal conditions but was occasionally used as a "sick room" in the event any of the children caught a communicable disease. The second floor of the laundry room was also used as an isolation ward.

The third major building (admin) was the original girls' house where we ate meals before 1942. It was converted into a study hall, main office and residence of the head mistress. It was where the first black and white television set was located. One of my early memories of mealtime was looking forward to breakfast. The little kids were given two pieces of bread spread with molasses, which soaked into the bread. Everyone loved it and it was used as a medium of exchange. "I'll give you three pieces of molasses bread if you will … " These were uncomplicated times.

Sister Lena Beideck was the head mistress from about 1913 until Sister Wilma Loehrig replaced her in 1942. Sister Lena was loved by most of the kids, but she did not run a tight ship. Tabor's reputation was less than stellar for producing kids that were not high school dropouts.

With the arrival of Sister Wilma, the Home became a lot more structured. No longer was it sufficient to "meet standards." Kids with talent were encouraged to strive for success in life. This was expected in academics as well as athletics. From the time she arrived in 1942 until she retired in 1971, it was assumed all Tabor kids would graduate from high school and apply for college or join the armed forces. It became unacceptable to drop out of school at age 16 and start working.

Life at Tabor was about acquiring survival skills as rapidly as possible so that wise decisions could be made with minimal discomfort. A pecking order was quickly established so you knew whom you could beat up and who could beat you up. But actually there was not much fighting once the ground rules were established. Acts of kindness regarding new arrivals at the home were few and far between. Your moniker was "new kid." That was how everyone addressed the novice. It could be weeks or months before others referred to you by your name. This probation period lasted until the next "new kid" arrived.

One of my earliest and most traumatic experiences occurred early in the school year of 1941. Changing schools in the third grade should have been seamless, because most material should have been covered in the first two years. But the Upper Darby school in suburban Philadelphia neither introduced cursive writing nor long division before school year three. I was the only child in grade three who was printing during writing class. I did not have a clue how to solve long division problems. My solution to the latter was to feign a stomach ache when the class was asked to divide. One day after being sent home, I found myself transported to a hospital in Philadelphia where they relieved me of my appendix. Even as a 7-year-old, I realized that some seemingly cunning solutions had unintended consequences.

Tabor Home cast of characters:

- Jake Highton: One of the positive role models at Tabor. Sports fanatic and journalism major at Penn State. First Tabor kid who attended college. Wrote sports for the Doylestown Intelligencer. Pretty good side-arm baseball pitcher, high jumper and starting end on the high school football team.
- Don (Fats) Allison: Colleague of Jake and one of the back-room guys. Came to Tabor as a slightly overweight child and, although possessing a normal build, carried the disparaging nickname. Good athlete and catcher on the baseball team.
- Brother Will: Natural athlete and the original "no-sweat" teenager. His philosophy in life was to exert only enough effort to skim over the bar. He always dated the prettiest girls in school and was everyone's favorite. He was just a couple of names from the "anchorman" when he graduated from the Naval Academy in 1958.
- Albert McGettigan: Pint-sized kid with a great singing voice.

- Don (Stilts) Fritz: One of the true orphans at Tabor. Obsessed with sports from the time he showed up in 1945 as a tall 9-year-old, someone remarked that he looked as if he were walking on stilts. The moniker stuck for about 10 years. Later in life he was named to the Central Bucks High School Hall of Fame as a four-sport athlete. He was a close friend of my brother Will.

- Walt Evans: The only child of a mother who had emigrated from Germany. He never lived down the fact that his mother commented that one day she would say, "Pack up Walter, we're going back to Germany." Anything associating a child with either Japan or Germany during World War II was the kiss of death. Walt was bright and had an excellent singing voice.

- The Hoppe boys: Family of three boys, who were often involved in any mischievous adventures at the home. Joe was the oldest and worked at the barn, milking the cows. Carl was athletic and disciplined and loved playing combat in the woods. (Jake Highton still has a scar on his hand when stabbed by Carl with a wooden bayonet when playing commandos in the Tabor woods.) Bobby (Toad) Hoppe was the baby and became a foreign missionary in later life.

- The Maloney sisters, Dorothea and Eleanor: Dotty was in my class throughout high school. She was always a huge fan of mine. She was a cheerleader in high school and among the most popular students in the class. Dotty was not one of Sister Wilma's favorites, primarily because the Sister favored boys over girls. Eleanor was several years younger and was often in hot water with the staff, because she exhibited such teenager characteristics as sullenness and flippancy.

To capture the essence of 10 years of life at Tabor in a single chapter is difficult, because it involved tears, great joy, laughter, cruelty, enduring friendship, fights, a realization life is not fair and first-hand knowledge of the class system. Tears were a common sight among the younger children as they tried to establish their manhood among their peers while remaining on the right side of the authorities. Great joy was in shorter supply, but was supplied by athletic success. Laughter was ubiquitous, as much of the time we were creating our own games of simulated combat and athletic competition. The older boys sometimes inflicted cruel treatment on the younger ones, such as unprovoked punching or snatching a favorite possession, although there were unspoken rules of engagement. Bullying to instill fear was not practiced, because there was a sense of symbiosis among all the children. Despite some amount of internal disagreement, any time Tabor kids came under fire, they would have the backing of every other Home kid. That sense of loyalty creates enduring friendships. It did not take long to catch on about life's inequality and that you had better play the cards you were dealt. Public school teachers, parents of friends and newspaper journalists reinforced one's position in the class system. Virtually every published article about a Tabor child or alumnus would always have the theme: Tabor kid makes good.

The older a child is when he begins his tenure at the Home, the less lasting impact it tends to have on his psyche and sense of self-worth. All children raised at Tabor suffered basic feelings of insecurity. They developed mechanisms to cope with being powerless in an adult world. But for those starting under the age of 6, it seemed particularly traumatic. A common trait exhibited by many of the kids was a tendency to admit a failure soon after meeting someone for the first time. Failing a test or being "left back" in school might be disclosed quickly. This not only disarmed the other person, but also was a protection against criticism.

The Edison Elementary School consisted of grades one through eight with the top three grades sharing one large dividable room. The American Legion awarded a medal to the eighth-grade student who was voted by the class to have contributed the most during the school year. Traditionally, the president of the class was given the honor, which happened to be me in 1947. Just before graduation, the principal conducted the voting with these preliminary remarks, "It is time to vote for the Legion award which will be presented during the commencement ceremonies. Vote for the person who has contributed the most for the class. I don't want you to vote for a deadhead like Wright." I had no idea why he thought I was a loser. The class followed his suggestion and voted for Bob Ott. He and Dorothea Maloney accepted the awards at graduation.

Bucks County sponsored standardized testing for all eighth graders in math, reading, spelling and English. One of the high school girls at Tabor, Josie, was working in the county office. One of her tasks was to grade and record scores of the various tests. She told me that I had scored the highest grade in both English and arithmetic. At the eighth grade graduation ceremony the $2.50 stipend for the highest average in arithmetic was awarded to me but the $5 English award was presented to Rosalind Case, a classmate. The school might have had a policy of not giving multiple awards. But it seemed quite unjust to me. The sad part of the story was that I wasn't surprised at the obvious bias on the part of the principal. I didn't take it personally. He felt that way about all the Tabor kids. I learned at an early age that life was not necessarily fair.

It is ironic that after several of his "doomed students" from Tabor were lauded for their athletic and scholastic achievements, the principal bragged to colleagues about "his boys" and the role he played in their development. An elementary school was named for him following his retirement. His obituary lionized him as a giant among Pennsylvania educators. But to us Tabor kids he was no giant.

It has been said that most people will die with the ability to recall only 10 memorable days in their lifetime. I could accept that observation only if large numbers of elderly people with advanced stages of Alzheimer's disease were included in the study. Any former Tabor kid can come up with 10 memorable childhood days in about 10 minutes time. And they do so with appropriate levels of humor, pathos and nostalgia.

A farmer who was a former Tabor resident, Harry (Boog) Burmeister, carried out the day-to-day management of the dairy and truck farm. He recruited one willing victim among the crop of teenage boys to assist in the milking of the cows and cleaning out the stables. The onus of finding a replacement was placed on the current victim in the event he wanted relief from his job. It was always unclear to me why anyone would volunteer for such an onerous job. But Fats Allison, Joe Hoppe and Don Fritz were the designated assistants during the 1940s. They seemed quite happy with their elevated status in life.

While the majority of the children had to get permission from Sister Wilma to leave the grounds for any extracurricular activity, the "barn boys" negotiated directly with the head farmer. Chores such as sweeping the pavements and driveways, hand mowing the acres of grass, making hay, shucking corn in the autumn, weeding the rows of vegetables, picking up potatoes and threshing wheat in the summer had to be completed in a satisfactory manner before leisure activities were permitted. It was a pragmatic control mechanism that worked effectively.

World War II started in December of 1941, several months after Will and I came to Tabor. The war had a significant impact on many of the children's day-to-day activities. Rationing of food and gasoline was a way of life. Several Dutch sailors spent a few weeks in rehabilitation at Tabor after their submarine was sunk off the Eastern coastline. Everyone was fascinated with the war, and events both in Europe and the Pacific theaters were followed with great interest. In mid-1942 when the Germans were trying to push the Russians off the Crimean peninsula into the Black Sea, Jake Highton and I were sitting on the rear seat on Tabor's bus returning from church one Sunday. We were pushing each other off the seat (Crimean peninsula) amid loud cries of victory. The bus driver, Joe Moskavitz, in his mid-20s, was the temporary assistant farmer. Halfway home Sister Wilma had Joe stop the bus and banished both the German and Russian gladiators from the vehicle, because our excessive noise was "upsetting Joe." The two war-weary combatants trudged the remaining half-mile home.

Living on the northern border of Tabor Home was a family whose youngest child, named Bruce, was a classmate at Edison. He lived in a two-story green house with an older brother George, and they kept a 10-acre truck farm and a small apple orchard. I suppose they would be classified today as working poor. They had little use for Tabor kids, and this was quite obvious in their demeanor. Perhaps there was some justification for their attitude toward the next-door thieves who occasionally stole their apples. In any case, there was no love lost regarding this family.

A relatively benign weapon that was commonly used by the young boys to shoot at birds and squirrels was a foot-long piece of inner tube attached by two strings to a small pouch, which held the stones. It was called a "slappie" and the range of the small rocks varied from about 20 to 75 yards. One morning Albert McGettigan and I decided to experiment with a two-man slappie that would have a range of 100 yards and hurl a two-pound rock. The basic flaw in the concept was that a coordinated maneuver involving the rapid lowering of the thumb was necessary in order to preclude the accelerating rock from striking the forward holder's thumb.

After the initial failure and the icing down of Al's swollen thumb, we went back to the drawing board and devised a giant sling shot, which minimized the probability of self-injury. After cutting down a small sapling which formed a large Y, we tied two bungee-like rubber strips to the small tree, creating a slingshot about six feet high and capable of hurling a fist-sized rock several hundred yards.

It did not occur to us that if this rock struck someone in the head, it could be lethal. We took our invention up to the far side of the woods and spotted George cultivating his field about 200 yards away. We aimed our contraption and watched as our rock followed a 45-degree arc, striking the shocked target in the leg.

As we were on the edge of the woods, we immediately abandoned our homemade weapon and high-tailed it back to safer ground. The now limping and furious neighbor went directly to Sister Wilma to report the incident and seek redress for the dastardly deed. She asked the complainant to identify the culprits so she could take action. He was unable to shed any light on the identification of the possible perpetrators, so she dismissed him with a shrug of her shoulders. This was not one of my finest hours. The potential injuries it could have inflicted on an innocent neighbor could not be justified.

On more than one occasion we would not be so fortunate in escaping detection for deeds most foul. The punishment that was most often meted out was standing on the stage in the dining room while everyone else ate dinner. I recall a specific incident where several of us were caught stealing pumpkins and our punishment was to consume the raw pumpkin on the stage in front of all the kids. The audience thought it was great fun.

Singing was always encouraged at Tabor. If you could carry a tune, it was expected you would sing in the Lutheran Church choir. The choir would practice once a week to prepare for the Sunday morning service. Both Will and I along with two or three other heavenly voices would walk the mile or so to the Lutheran Church on Thursday evenings and prepare for the weekend festivities. Walter Evans and Albert McGettigan were colleagues with quite good singing voices. The problem with Evansie was that he couldn't do anything right. I often punched him on the arm to express my displeasure at his being a quintessential "screw-up," which I felt reflected badly on all Tabor kids.

He seemed helpless to change, however. One night as we returned home from choir practice, God smiled on us as we passed

Lewis' Atlantic gas station south of town. The owner had forgotten to lock the outdoor cooler, and it was full of soft drinks. We all helped ourselves and consumed them as we proceeded on foot down Route 611, which led between Doylestown and Tabor, congratulating ourselves on our good fortune. Unbeknown to us, a neighbor had seen us and reported the theft to the local police, who responded within several minutes. As their squad car pulled up, the lead law enforcement officer inquired as to whether we had seen anyone taking bottles of soda pop from the gas station. As you might expect, we denied it, aghast that he would accuse us of such a heinous crime. After all, we were members of the church choir and had been singing the Lord's praises just minutes before.

The sound of Evansie's half-consumed soft drink bottle breaking on the macadam highway interrupted our plea of innocence and acted like a starter's pistol at a track meet. As we fled toward the inviting cornfield just a hundred yards away, we all denounced the day Walter Evans showed up at Tabor. The cops tried to scare us out of the darkened cornfield with a loud threat of shooting into the field. We could barely contain our laughter. All members of the angelic choir crept home after Doylestown's finest gave up and drove away.

Of all of the holidays, Christmas meant the most to Tabor kids. All the local charities seemed to band together and contribute gifts, money, clothes and candy to the Home. Every year we received from the Emergency Police an individual box containing an orange surrounded with hard candy. We loved it, because most of the year there was a distinct shortage of luxuries that most children take for granted.

Friehofer's bakery would deliver bread and rolls to Tabor on a daily basis. The driver would sell day-old pastries to the kids for 5 cents. Purchasing six sticky buns for a nickel was the closest thing to Nirvana that most of the children ever experienced. The excitement that a nickel in your pocket could command, while waiting for the bakery truck, was unbelievable.

On your 12th birthday you joined the Boy Scouts. Nearly every Tabor boy was a member of the Edison troop. It meant weekly meetings, summer camp, projects to attain merit badges and occasional community events. One learned a variety of skills that increased your confidence to survive in the woods. Jake Highton attained the rank of Eagle Scout, but most of the rest of us dropped out of the program before we earned the required merit badges. I was short two merit badges before high school sports took priority. Nevertheless, I retain fond memories of my years in scouting. I always knew that I could survive in the wild, which was of great benefit in my military life during events like survival training.

Sports played a significant part in the life of every boy at Tabor. In the first place, it was an all-hands requirement to play softball after dinner if weather conditions permitted. Sister Viola, a diminutive taskmaster in charge of the boy's house, was the pitcher for both sides. She was a sports aficionado from Ohio and a big Buckeye's fan during football season. Constant practice honed athletic skills that would pay off in later years as Tabor kids excelled in high school sports programs.

Jake Highton was in the vanguard. He started as end on the football team. He was also a high jumper and middle distance runner on the track team. If there was a common bond among us, it was an obsession with sports. We each collected baseball cards, knew all the rules of the game cold, memorized batting averages of major league players and dreamed of eventually earning a living playing big league baseball. It was the equivalent of attending one of Nick Bollettieri's tennis camps in Florida. You either mastered the skills or were humiliated in the process of failing.

National Farm School (which became Delaware Valley College) was a two-year agricultural college about two and one-half miles from Tabor. It produced exciting, hard-nosed single-wing football teams. Every Saturday we would make the trek by the back road to watch Farm School humiliate the opposing team. We also made use of their gym to practice basketball during the winter months when snow prevented us from using the outdoor court in back of the boys' house. We thought nothing of walking the five-miles round trip. The really hard task was carrying a leather basketball for three miles and not bouncing it on the muddy road en route to the indoor courts. My dad was a staunch supporter of any of our athletic endeavors. He kept us supplied with basketballs, footballs and baseball equipment.

Incidentally, he never failed to visit us on Sunday afternoons, riding the bus from Philadelphia. It was a stabilizing influence on my life during those days when cosmic forces seemed to be in control of my fate. It was quite sad to observe about 50 percent of the kids who looked longingly on those lucky enough to have parents visit on the weekends.

If present-day child psychologists observed some of the discipline techniques used they would be aghast. Lynford (Lympy) Disque, an incorrigible 7-year-old, was actually given coal in his Christmas stocking and nothing else. Among other deeds, Lympy had captured a chicken from the coup behind the boy's house and had buried it alive. I'm not sure the punishment fit the crime, but the Sisters were quite pragmatic about discipline. They would eventually find some means of convincing you to follow the rules. There was relatively little sympathy and a minimum of love given to anyone, as that was considered impractical with five or six permanent staff to serve 80 or so children.

Of my four years in high school, the first period lasted three years and consisted of average to below-average performance. It is a scenario that is not unlike a great many children trying to find themselves in a strange environment and muddling their way through school without defined goals. It is not that I didn't try to excel. A competitive spirit has always been part of my makeup. But, after the successes in elementary school (class president, successful athlete, smarter than most kids in the class), it seemed logical that good fortune would follow me to the next scholastic level. In fact, I struggled in Latin and actually failed Algebra I. This from the kid who won the award in eighth grade for the highest average in arithmetic. I almost felt obliged to give back the $2.50.

But those first three years of high school also included some successes. I was selected as home room representative one year, kicked for the junior varsity (JV) football team, started for the JV basketball team as a junior and managed to earn a varsity "D" in baseball. I felt the pinnacle was having the opportunity to play in Shibe Park in Philadelphia (major league baseball stadium) for the Eastern Pennsylvania championship in 1949 as part of the 15-year-and-under American Legion Midget League.

Although I was not a stellar football player, I played right halfback for the varsity and scored several touchdowns during the season. About halfway through the football season, the seniors voted for class officers. Our class president the previous year was Virginia James, and she had moved away in 1950, so the election was wide open. It probably helped that I was a varsity football player and a reasonably good public speaker. I wasn't too surprised that the class elected me president. But one of the teachers was overheard to say: "God help us. They've elected a

FOOTBALL player to lead the class."

Basketball was more to my liking, and I was fortunate enough to break the Bux-Mont league scoring record and was selected to the all-league first team. To cap off the season, the team elected me captain and the senior class voted me most popular and best athlete, quite an honor for a Tabor Home kid.

In retrospect, two things that were missing from Tabor Home life were a feeling of being loved and strong role models to give assistance in life counseling. I never developed intellectual curiosity as a child. Education and training were barriers that had to be hurdled. I studied to get good grades, not to absorb facts or understand the philosophy of life. Everyone was lonely. It was part of growing up. You faced the day and put problems like loneliness on the back burner.

In all fairness, it was a nearly impossible task to raise all children successfully. A study by an evaluation team would probably award the Tabor staff fairly high marks.

Orv Wright and his younger brother Wilbur came to Tabor Home in 1941 and remained there for 10 years. He graduated from the U.S. Naval Academy and retired from the Navy after 23 years. He is the father of four children and lives with his second wife Carolyn in Owego, N.Y. He is past president of the Owego Rotary Club and teaches several courses to foster children under the auspices of Tabor Children's Services.

AM I ONLY REMEMBERING THE GOOD TIMES?
By Arnold Wenzloff

As I think back 50 or 60 years ago, some specific events are quite clear and vivid, while most of the things I experienced in those 14 years I spent at the Home are vague impressions until someone else refreshes my memory. Here are some of the highlights that come to mind:

- Many happy hours swimming in the pool. Sometimes the green algae darkened the water so much you could swim up to a girl underwater and pinch her and remain undetected.

- Devising ways to appropriate food and drink which was kept under lock and key. We became quite adept at forcing the pantry window open and sending in a small body to recover any goodies stored there. Little guys were also useful for riding the dumbwaiter down to the storerooms where canned juices were stored.

- There were 16 steps connecting the back room to the large bathroom on the first floor.

- The closet at the top of the steps was used to store barn clothes, which did not have a very pleasing aroma.

- I remember Evansie (Walter Evans) was often the butt of practical jokes. One time someone cut the bottoms out of his pajamas so that when he put them on, his butt was exposed.

- The basketball court in back of the boys' house was in constant use. The area right under the basket was a closet that was used to store May Day dishes. Because of the excessive body-checking under the basket, the sound of breaking crockery was a common sound. Sister Wilma never did solve the puzzle of how so many May Day dishes failed to survive in the storage closet.

- Tabor Home in the 1940s was not a genteel environment with loving and supportive peers. For a young boy it was a trial-and-error existence with not much room for slow learners. I remember a rotten log located close to the softball field that was full of bees. A group of teen-aged boys convinced an 8-year-old to don a makeshift costume of burlap bags and retrieve the honey that the bees had so painstakingly produced. The evil masterminds armed the victim with a hatchet to facilitate removal of the coveted honey. The end result was predictable. The 8-year-old received multiple stings and learned a much-needed lesson. The teenagers ended up too close to the action and were also stung on the run. All's well that ends well. Some modicum of justice was served.

- One of my fondest memories was sledding in the winter. There was sloping terrain in back of the barn that we called Nutcracker Hill. We would amass multiple sleds, holding the feet of the person on the sled in front, in a long line and veer right and left on the way down the slope. The sleds at the end of the "whip" would inevitably careen out of control into the creek. Great fun!

Upon reflection I sometimes wonder if I am only remembering the good times?

Arnie started at Tabor in late 1941 at the age of 4. He remained there until he graduated from Central Bucks High School 14 years later. In recent years Arnie lived in Florida with his partner Esther until his death in November 2005 of a heart-related illness.

PLEASE DON'T THROW ME IN THE BRIAR PATCH
By Catherine Kniese Choromanski

The Kniese family was living on Hamilton Street in Doylestown until my parents got divorced in 1941. With my mother trying to raise a family of four children on a minimum wage salary, it soon became evident that her only viable solution was to make the children wards of the state. So in 1942, Charles (age 10), Cathy (me, age 8), and Bob (age 7), were driven down Route 611 to Tabor Home for Children. Butch, the baby of the family, had to remain with mother until he turned 5 in 1943, at which time he was permitted to join his siblings.

I distinctly recall how displeased and angry I was upon being enrolled. But when Sister Wilma called over one of the girls to show me around, my pain dissipated rather quickly. That girl was Marie Knauss, and she became my best friend at Tabor along with Eleanor Maloney.

The memories that stand out were the fun times with all the kids, as well as the holidays that were clearly the highpoints of life in the Home. May Day was always a blast with booths selling all kinds of wares and people from town and Tabor alumni visiting and telling what it was like in the old days.

Most of the kids felt Christmas was magic, because we got presents from people we didn't even know, such as board members, police organizations and church groups. The stage was full of goodies which were in real short supply 51 weeks of the year. We loved getting stockings loaded with candy canes and other stuff on Christmas morning.

Easter was another holiday that brought free candy to the Home. I think a store in Doylestown would donate a huge chocolate and coconut Easter egg to Tabor after it was on display in their store window. We loved it!

Occasionally, we would get into trouble with the authorities. One time I remember Sara Duckworth eating in the boys' backyard next to the pool. I asked her what she was munching on, and she told me molasses on apple slices and was it good! When we found out that she had obtained the molasses from the basement of Sister Wilma's building (admin), we made plans to appropriate the wonderful snack. I remember that Emily Mumaw, Sara Duckworth, Sandy Walton and I were among the warriors that went forth to free the imprisoned food.

After a successful daring raid in which we ate our fill, Sandy's conscience started working overtime and she confessed our sin to Sister Wilma. Our punishment for the heinous crime was that, for the next week, our entire diet would consist of nothing but molasses bread. Since that was my very favorite food, I could not help but think of the fable about Br'er Rabbit begging not to be thrown into the briar patch.

Another amusing incident I recall involved several of us girls tying Eleanor Maloney to her bed one night and watching her get a whipping when Sister Emma caught her. I'm sure El was not happy with the turn of events, as she was the victim twice.

Reflecting upon my days at Tabor I would conclude that Sister Wilma did about as good a job as she could with all her responsibilities. There were things I didn't like, such as weeding the endless rows of potatoes in the 17-acre patch and scrubbing the kitchen floors. But I learned some homemaking skills such as canning, which came in very handy later in life.

My best memories were all the fun I had with kids my own age. My worst remembrances were not having a mother to tuck me in, hug me and tell me bedtime stories. My mother did visit us every Sunday, and I am grateful for that. Several years before we left Tabor, Sister Wilma encouraged us to attend the Methodist Church in Doylestown and spend Sunday afternoon with our mother. Little acts of kindness meant a lot to Tabor kids.

Cathy Kniese came to Tabor Home in 1942 when she was 8 years old, along with her older brother Charles and younger brother Bob. A year later her 5-year-old brother Butch (James) joined the clan. Charles left in 1948; Cathy, Bob and Butch left in 1949. Cathy presently lives in Trenton, N.J.

MY OVERRIDING GOAL
WAS TO LEAVE TABOR HOME
By Walter Evans

My life at Tabor Home was an unmitigated nightmare. I was bullied from the first day my mother and I took the Number 22 bus from Glenside, Pa., in 1941, arrived at the big house and met Sister Lena. She sent me over to the boys' house with my suitcase where I met the Wright brothers, two of the Hoppe boys and Eddie Knauss. One of them snatched my hat and started a game of keep-away. In short order I was in tears and my sentence had hardly begun. Almost immediately I was given the name Sprockets because of my glasses, and I wore that moniker for years.

I am not sure exactly why I was targeted. It could have been because my mother had come from Germany and expressed a desire to return. Or perhaps it was that I was quite klutzy in sports. Whatever the reason, I definitely wore a bulls-eye shirt for much of my youth, and it had a long-term negative effect on my self-esteem and desire to succeed in life.

For some reason, it took me a long time to figure out the formula for successful living. At Tabor, not getting caught at breaking the rules was very important for a successful life. It seems that I never mastered that axiom. Case in point: One summer day several of us went down to the "rocks" in Edison, and we decided to set a small plastic boat on fire and watch it burn and sink. The only problem was that we had no matches to torch the sails. I volunteered to run over to a small store in Edison to buy the matches. While purchasing the fire sticks, the local Justice of the Peace, Squire Wrigley, happened to be in the store. He inquired where I lived and what my plans were for the matches. I quickly replied that I lived at Tabor Home and Sister Wilma had sent me down here for the matches. Having successfully bamboozled the local arm of the law, I returned to the "rocks" and we carried out our plan to sink the Titanic.

On our way home, we passed the Justice-of-the-Peace's office. He signaled for me to come in, which I reluctantly did. He told me he had called Sister Wilma, that she knew nothing about the purchase of matches, and that she would be waiting for an explanation when I got home. For the indiscretion I was given a whipping and sentenced to stand on the stage while everyone else (including my cohorts in crime) ate dinner.

Even though it appeared that I had to wear the loser hat again, the incident actually was a positive event. I realized that the little lie I told was not worth the penalty. To this day, I am truthful to a fault. I resolved never to lie again.

A second event in my youth may give the reader some insight into my inability to cope with the complex methodology necessary to be successful in the underworld. A group of Tabor kids had just finished a required class in catechism so we could become members of the Lutheran Church. As we made our way on foot back home, one of our group discovered that the gas station on Main Street had failed to lock their soda dispenser. What could we do? God had smiled on us and was offering us a free treat for being good Christians. We helped ourselves and proceeded south on Route 611 toward home when a police cruiser pulled up and asked us if we had any knowledge about a gang of kids that were stealing soft drinks. As we were proclaiming our innocence, the half-consumed bottle of pop slipped out of my hand and shattered on the cement highway with a resounding crash.

As if responding to a starter's pistol, my fellow perpetrators dashed into a cornfield across the highway. Not being a natural athlete, I was collared and forced to pay for all four sodas. The cops dropped me off at the main gate, so Sister Wilma never found out about our run-in with the local police.

The downside of being a victim is not only the humiliation that is experienced on a daily basis but also the "piling on" by authority figures. I felt that both Sister Wilma and the principal of the elementary school showed zero compassion for a child that desperately needed support. For instance, I won the elementary school's Gross Awards for outstanding math and spelling several times but never received any congratulations from anyone. And the principal suspended me for no apparent reason and told me to bring my mother or Sister Wilma to school if I wanted to return to classes.

It has been said that any experience that does not kill you, makes an individual stronger. I'm not sure I am ready to sign up for that, but I did leave the Home with a life-long love for animals, a deep-seated belief in God, and the realization that music would play a significant role in my life. That was balanced with an equally strong belief that I could not be successful in life and a self-esteem evaluation that was as low as the grading curve went.

Why would any child that was beat up almost every day believe in God? In addition to the daily devotions and prayers that were conducted at Tabor, there was always a religious aura that influenced the children in daily living. I remember hitchhiking to town to catch the bus to Philadelphia to visit my mom one weekend. She had given me a dollar for carfare, but it disappeared somewhere between Tabor and town. In despair, I stood outside a local church and prayed for help. I sat at the bus station with my head in my hands when a stranger approached and asked what my problem was. When I relayed my sad tale to him, he asked if I were running away. I denied it, of course, and gave him Sister Wilma's telephone number. After calling her, he took a dollar out of his wallet and wished me well. To this day, I am convinced that that stranger was a messenger from God.

The two strengths in my life were both inherited, a good singing voice and high intelligence. My voice allowed me to sing in the church choir, excel in the glee club in high school and be selected for both county and district chorus. The director of the high school chorus, Miss Richmond, let me direct the boys' chorus in the spring concert. That was heady stuff for a "loser" from Tabor Home.

It took me a long time to realize that I was smart. I scored so high on my aptitude test for the Air Force that I was permitted to select any training they offered. I chose electronics. Later in life I was tested for intelligence and scored high enough to qualify for the Mensa organization. I finally got my college degree in 1969 and turned my life around.

I know my tale of growing up at Tabor Home is not an uplifting one. I have horrible memories of those 10 years, and left a very angry and confused man. Yet, through it all, I survived and found a great deal of insight into my values, and myself, and realized I am contributing to society. And, life is very, very precious to me. By the way, I have forgiven my tormentors.

Walt Evans came to Tabor at age 6 in the summer of 1941 and left more than 10 years later after graduating from Central Bucks High School. He lives in Cheltenham, Pa., with his wife Carol.

TABOR WAS THE BEST DECISION
OUR FATHER MADE
By Richie Knauss

My family was living in Philadelphia until our mother deserted us and left our dad with four children under the age of 8. As a bartender who worked nights, he had limited options regarding our care and feeding. So, in early 1942 our father requested that all four of his children be placed into Tabor Home. We were all quite worried that our family might be separated, but that didn't happen. I remember as a 5-year-old, the first day at Tabor was pretty scary.

As it turned out, it was the best thing that he ever did for us. In looking back, growing up in Bucks County on a farm with 80 children was most enjoyable.

When I describe to friends what a children's home was like, they have a hard time accepting the fact that it was a nice place to live, especially with the control that Sister Wilma had on all the kids regarding leaving the grounds. But, as with all systems, there are ways to bend rules without breaking them.

My older brother Eddie must have missed that lesson, because he didn't adjust very well to authority and was asked to leave the Home well before graduating from high school.

It has always been puzzling to me why some kids adjust to a regimented environment and others have a difficult time. One key, I believe, is how good an athlete one is. I was blessed with natural athletic talent and was able to fit in very easily at Tabor. By the time I got to high school, I played on the varsity football and basketball teams and played American Legion baseball in the summer. A sport not only kept you out of trouble, but the self-discipline necessary to play the game well was often transferred to other aspects of your life.

I would probably be described as a "straight arrow" growing up. I was seldom in trouble, but I did not have a perfect record. I remember making an unauthorized phone call to my girl friend from the phone located in the locked pantry storeroom and getting caught by Sister Wilma. That mistake caused me to be restricted to the grounds for a month. You often have to pay a steep price for true love! Another time I put a dummy in my bed and made my way to Doylestown to spend some quality time with my girlfriend. Her parents returned earlier than expected and found us on the front couch watching television. They were not pleased and informed Sister Wilma of my nocturnal visit. The hammer came down and I was awarded another 30-day grounding. My image as that "nice Knauss boy" was starting to tarnish.

Working on the Tabor farm was a mixed bag. I didn't mind the barn work (although I never milked the cows) or baling hay. But weeding rows of potatoes so long that you couldn't see the end or husking corn in freezing weather was another story. No one could like that type of work.

We used to walk over to National Farm School and watch their football team play on Saturdays during the season. On occasion, these scheduled football games would conflict with corn husking time. I recall departing the cornfield early with a couple of other football fans and hightailing it over to Farm School to catch the second half. By the time we got there, Boog Burmeister, the Tabor Home farmer, was waiting in his pickup in a non-negotiating mood, and transported us back to the field. He obviously had seen Tabor kids in action before.

My adult friends, influenced by Oliver Twist, believe that kids raised in a children's home are, most likely, headed for jail. Well, it just ain't so!

Richie came to Tabor in early 1942 with three siblings, Marie, Eddie and Ted. He remained there until graduating from Central Bucks in 1955. He retired in 1999 and lives in Morganton, N.C., with his wife Diann.

I AM PROUD TO HAVE BEEN A TABOR HOME BOY
By Don Fritz

After spending most of my early childhood in foster homes in Pennsylvania and New Jersey, I was living in a foster home in Akron, Pa., a town located about 55 miles west of Philadelphia, when the decision was made to send me to Tabor Home to join my sister Billie Jane. We were the only actual orphans at Tabor, even though some local people often referred to the Home as the orphanage.

That September evening in 1945 was quite memorable, even after 59 years. I met Sister Wilma in the administrative building, and she escorted me over to the boys' house and turned me over to Sister Viola, a diminutive boys' supervisor, whose passion in life was sports.

At age 11, I was a head taller than other children my age. So when the 26-bed front room had no vacancies, Sister Viola decided to bunk me in the 10-bed room with the older boys. At the time I did not realize that moving to the "back room" was a rite of passage to which every kid aspired. For the next 10 years, that was my home.

As I was undressing for bed that night, someone said, "Look at that new kid. He has the longest legs. He looks like he's walking on stilts." The name stuck and for the next ten years I answered to Stilts. Even today, some kids from Tabor or old friends from Doylestown call me by my childhood nickname. In those days, many kids received nicknames like Toad, Meathead, or Sprockets, but until someone else arrived, they were only known as New Kid.

I have many fond memories of my years at Tabor, too many to relate in a single story. I liked the idea that we were not self-sufficient but relied on the public school system for education. We all attended the Lutheran Church in Doylestown and received spiritual guidance from both inside and outside the Home. Some kids were more successful than others in absorbing the guidance.

There was clearly a double standard regarding supervision of the boys and girls, and perhaps that was necessary. The boys were pretty well on their own, most of the time. After chores were completed, we did just about anything we wanted to, as long as it was legal. That rule was followed most of the time, but not always.

I could make a long list of kids' names that were there in my 10-year span, but I won't since I don't want to slight anyone in case I forget one or two. My classmates in elementary and high school were Will Wright, Carl Hoppe, Catherine Kniese and Pat Oxinio. Of the five of us, only Pat left the Home before graduating from Central Bucks High School.

Within a year of arriving at Tabor, I was given the dubious honor of being selected to take Bill Beck's job at the barn. Becky left the Home prematurely and ended up joining the Navy. Usually one boy was the designated "barn boy," and his duties consisted of milking the cows twice a day and mucking out the stalls daily. The barn odor seemed to remain on one's clothes for some time after the daily chores were complete. I worked under the supervision of Harry (Boog) Burmeister, a former Tabor boy, who came back to the Home in the 1930s and was hired in 1940 as the full-time farmer and handy man.

During the growing and harvesting seasons, all the boys assisted in routine farm work. We had vegetables to weed and pick, wheat to thresh, and hay to cut, rake, pitch on the wagon, and transport to the multi-story mow in the barn. We also grew 17 acres of potatoes, which had to be harvested every year. There was always plenty of farm work to go around. The girls assisted with some of the farming tasks, such as weeding the truck patch and the potato plants that seemed to go on for miles. For the most part, the girls had inside chores that included cleaning, food preparation and canning of fruits and vegetables.

I think the Home kids learned a good work ethic while growing up there. Some didn't work as hard as others, but we all worked. After the chores were completed, we played sports. It was almost mandatory to participate. We played football, basketball and baseball at Tabor, in Doylestown and at Farm School. In addition, we fished, hiked and went to movies at the County Theater. Most of our spare time was used to the fullest.

I really liked Tabor Home. It was the first real home I ever had, and of the 10 years I spent there, about 90 percent of the time I remember as good. Two holidays especially come to mind when reminiscing about good times, Christmas and May Day.

There was nothing like Christmas at Tabor. Presents were piled high, from one end of the stage in the girls' house to the other. Every child had many gifts and, of course, we had good Christmas dinners. The service clubs in Doylestown would give parties for the kids starting about two weeks before Christmas Eve. The State Police would give us oranges and the police associations would draw names and present gifts to individuals. All holidays were celebrated with great meals.

May Day was also a special day for us. The ladies' auxiliary presented the sauerkraut dinner, and outside guests would be invited to participate in the festivities. There were booths set up on the grounds, and all sorts of wares were sold for the benefit of the Home. Many Tabor alumni would show up, and the kids were always pleased to see them.

To this day, I am proud to have been a Tabor Home boy. I learned so many things from the people who staffed the place as well as from people in Doylestown and the surrounding area. I credit Tabor Home for preparing me to become the man that I am today. To me, it will always be my home, my roots and my friend.

Don joined his older sister Billie Jane at Tabor Home in the autumn of 1945 and left 10 years later after graduating from high school. He lives in Chalfont, Pa., with his wife Martha. Don was inducted into the Central Bucks High School Athletic Hall of Fame in 2000.

I JUST GOT TIRED OF BEING TOLD WHAT TO DO!
By Jane Fritz Tindall

The Fritz family was fairly large even by pre-World War II standards. It consisted of four girls and two boys. I was the youngest girl and had only brother Don below me in the pecking order. I considered myself a tomboy because of my choice in clothes (sweaters and jeans) and the fact that I had a tough exterior. I never let anyone push me around.

Both my parents died while I was young, and the children were farmed out to relatives or sent to live with foster families. My brother Don and I ended up at Tabor Home in the autumn of 1945, although I arrived a month or so before him. I was 14 years old at the time.

My memories of my two years at the Home are not very precise. I really can't remember how I felt when I arrived or what my state of mind was. I do recall living in a four-girl room on the second floor of the girls' house with Marie Knauss and Sara Duckworth. There were 40 girls living on one floor, and we shared one giant bathroom. You can imagine what it was like in the morning trying to get ready for breakfast with 39 other girls.

I used to get teased unmercifully by the Tabor boys and hated it. I wasn't mentally prepared to handle all the wisecracks from the immature troublemakers.

I felt quite protective of Don who was small and skinny. On more than one occasion I ended up fighting his battles, because I couldn't stand to see him hurt. He grew pretty tall in that first year and could finally look after himself.

My tendency to solve interpersonal problems physically often resulted in strained relationships. Two cases come to mind. One day Marie Knauss and I went down to a local restaurant, Roadside Rest, and purchased a Jewish pickle to eat that night in bed. That evening we were laughing and eating our snack when Sister Emma stormed into our room wielding a coat hanger. She told us to be quiet or she would use the hanger on our bottoms. I jumped out of bed and chased her down the hall back to her room while advising her to change her attitude or I would floor her. She never reported the incident to Sister Wilma who was in charge of Tabor.

A second incident occurred toward the end of my stay at the Home. My hair was in curlers one day, and Sister Wilma came up to me and grabbed me by the hair and started yelling at me. I told her to let go or I would punch her in the stomach. She complied with my request but continued yelling that I was setting a bad example for the younger girls by smoking and teaching them about sex. The truth was that I was completely naive and totally incapable of giving girls any advice regarding boys. But I received the tongue-lashing nevertheless.

There were a lot of fun times at Tabor with all the kids available to hang around with. I enjoyed the girls' parties, talking on the swings and the occasional dances. I distinctly remember one of the older boys, Jake Highton, teaching me how to waltz. It was one of the few times at Tabor that I felt like a princess, if for only several minutes.

Of course there were a lot of bumps in the road. Daily chores consisted of cleaning up the dining room, washing dishes and assisting the cook in the kitchen. I just got tired of being told what to do all the time and ran away to Philadelphia on two occasions to my grandmother's house. She sent me back each time.

Even though I was never a good student in school, when the principal informed me that he was not going to pass me to the ninth grade, I told him to pass me out the door. I started working as a domestic at Tabor, cleaning and cooking until I decided to get a job and my own apartment. That ended my association with Tabor Home.

I married Raymond Tindall in 1952, started my own family and have been married 53 years.

Jane Fritz arrived at Tabor in 1945 and left two years later at age 16. She has two sons and a daughter and lives in Maple Shade, N.J., with her husband Raymond.

I MARRIED A TABOR KID
By Martha Moyer Fritz

We were living in Baltimore, Md., and my dad was working in the chemical industry for a defense contractor. After my grandfather died, his 109-acre dairy farm in Chalfont, Pa., passed to my father, Ted Moyer, and his brother Enos. Uncle Enos was not making a profitable living farming and needed my dad's help. That is how I ended up in rural Bucks County as a farmer's daughter right after World War II.

Being raised on a dairy farm was an ideal setting for a young girl. I enjoyed all aspects of the farm from the animals to feeding and bedding the cows to projects with the 4-H club. My dad, who earned a Ph.D., was a progressive farmer and ran a modern dairy farm: He had automatic milking machines and an automated "mucking" machine that did the dirty work. Unlike me, my younger brother Richard hated everything about the farm and could not wait to graduate high school and flee the homestead.

After attending one- and two-room elementary schools in New Britain Township, I continued my education in the ninth grade in Doylestown High School. The school was built in 1912 and was outdated. The following year (1952) a brand new high school, Central Bucks, opened for business. It was a large school, and you didn't get to know everyone in your class. I met several girls from Tabor Home, but there was nothing out of the ordinary about them. They were just girls who happened to live in a children's home. However, everyone seemed to know and admire the Tabor boys, because they were the super athletes for the football, basketball, baseball and track teams.

Toward the end of my sophomore year, I attended a girl-scout troop meeting. Afterwards two or three of us decided to drive over to Tracy Greenholt's house and join a party. We knew there would be many of our friends attending. Tracy's parents were in the house but were not visible most of the evening. That party was memorable because I met Don Fritz from Tabor Home, one of the top athletes in high school. He was larger than life and seemed to be friends with everyone he met.

Don was several years older than me and had convinced Sister Wilma, head matron at Tabor Home, that he needed a driver's license so he could qualify for several jobs around town. That party evening Don had borrowed a car from a friend. I agreed to go riding with him. We ended up listening to a ball game on the car radio. At 10 p.m., when it was time to go home, the car's battery failed. The engine would not turn over, and we were stuck. Fortunately, Ben Haskey, a friend, happened to show up. He gave us a push to the New Britain train station where I reluctantly called my mother to explain why I wasn't home.

"Hello, Mom. I know it's late but can you give me a ride home from the New Britain train station? It's a long story but I was out with a boy that you have never heard of and the car broke down and we had to get towed to the train station and we were just listening to the ball game and ... "

I was grounded for an indeterminate period of time. Don took Gerry Myers to the Junior Prom. (He had already asked her before we met.) Don was officially persona non grata at 184 Moyer Road in Chalfont.

He graduated from Central Bucks High School that spring and got a temporary job that entailed driving around the county. He worked his charm with my parents, and they finally succumbed. We ended up spending a lot of time together that summer.

Don enrolled at Delaware Valley College in the fall of 1954. His love for football was greater than his love for the academic curriculum. Because Don had not taken a college preparatory course in high school, college-level work was quite challenging. After football season he dropped out of school and got a full-time job. My dad offered to fund his college education with the stipulation that he concentrate on studies and not play ball. Don rejected his offer even though he appreciated it.

Meanwhile, Don was living at Tabor. By this time I had a car and a curfew. I became quite adept at making the Tabor-to-Chalfont run in five minutes flat. I also got more involved with activities at Tabor Home. The two most memorable events were Christmas and May Day.

I had a very happy childhood and a marvelous home life, but visiting Tabor at Christmas made a lasting impression on me. A huge decorated tree dominated the stage in the dining room of the girls' dormitory. There were tons of wrapped gifts of every size and shape. The whole atmosphere was one of excitement, smiling faces and a constant buzz of anticipation. Life at Tabor may not have been a bowl of cherries for 50 weeks a year, but at Christmas there was magic in the air.

May Day was another time that most Tabor kids would

highlight as special. Booths were set up by merchants to sell their wares (I would sell rhubarb from our garden); the kids would put on plays for the public; and a ham and potato salad supper was on offer for a token amount. Tabor alumni would return to the Home and share stories of what it was like in the real world. All in all, there was a carnival-like atmosphere at Tabor the third weekend in May.

A similar supper, open to the public, was offered in October each year. The menu was pork and sauerkraut, and it was a big favorite among the local populace, including me.

The year 1955 was a significant one in my life. Don joined the Army in March, I graduated from Central Bucks in June and we got engaged later that month. When the government shipped my fiance off to Germany six months later, I knew I had to take action. Writing and receiving letters are not a substitute for being with your one and only. I convinced my mother and aunt to accompany me to Germany to witness my marriage to the Tabor kid, Don Fritz. My plan was to stay for just three weeks, return home and save money until Don returned in 1958. The three-week plan stretched into a full year, and we came back together on the same troop ship after Don's enlistment was over.

By the mid-60s, Don was approached to join a group of Tabor alumni that met monthly for social get-togethers. It was made up primarily of older people that had been at the Home prior to World War II. People like Fred Strowig, George Stafford and his sisters Ida Stafford Fenstermacher, Sarah Stafford Walker and Helen Stafford Vandegrift, Walter Trettin and John Frankenfield were the core people in the formation of the alumni meetings. It evolved into an association, and I served as their treasurer. We had a hard time recruiting younger alumni who did not seem to want to join the group. The reunion attendees peaked in 2004 when about 90 alumni came back to re-dedicate a portrait of Sister Lena Beideck, a beloved head matron at Tabor for about 30 years. For many it was the first time back at Tabor since they departed. Some brought their children or grandchildren along to see the place where they spent so much of their youth.

Here are some reflections after being married to Don for more than 48 years:

- From an outsider's viewpoint I have come to love Tabor and a good many of the people who grew up there.

- One of my favorite pastimes is to listen to Tabor stories when a group of alumni get together. No matter how often I hear them, I never tire of these tales. I was delighted when the Tabor Memories project took shape. I know it will interest more people than just the alumni. The stories and associated real-life drama are compelling and will fascinate readers.

- Even though children's homes have virtually disappeared, I am convinced a well-run institution is far superior to foster care. It gives a more stable environment and the caregivers are not doing it for any financial gain. My husband was an orphan, and he was in a series of foster families before he went to Tabor Home where he spent 11 of the best years of his life.

- Many Tabor kids disliked some of the staff at the Home. However, I can speak from experience when I state that I wasn't too fond of my parents during my teenage years. I give Tabor Home a lot of credit for doing a good job in raising their children, and I certainly don't envy the Sisters who took care of the children.

- There are exceptions, but most alumni look back on Tabor as having been, if not the greatest place to have been raised, at least a place where they knew they would be cared for. It was also someplace where "brothers and sisters" surrounded them and that they will remember those friendships for life.

Martha Fritz was not a Tabor Home alumna but has been married to Don Fritz for more than 48 years. She is the mother of three boys and lives in Chalfont, Pa., with her husband Don, who is retired.

I WAS GLAD TO LEAVE, BUT I DID MISS THE KIDS
By James Kniese

My earliest memory of Tabor Home was getting off the Number 22 PTC (Philadelphia Transit Company) bus at the big black gate and seeing my brothers and sister running down the sidewalk to greet me. They had been living at the Home for a full year before I was permitted to join them. It might seem strange for a 4-year-old to want to leave his mother, but I missed other family members so much. I could hardly wait for my fifth birthday so I could join them. I still remember that I was dressed in a brown and white coat and a beanie cap. I doubt that I was aware of the "big adventure" I was about to embark on.

It seemed that life consisted of going to school, working and leisure time. The first thing a young child would notice about Tabor was that there were so many kids to play with. I seem to remember that, despite the large number of kids, we were often bored with little to do. Of course, at certain times of the year there was too much to do. Weeding the 17-acre potato field was one example of too much work to accomplish. When we got the chance to pick beans at Farm School and be paid for it, we jumped at the chance. There weren't many ways to earn money at Tabor, but that was one.

Our chores were varied and quite different from those experienced in a middle class home. For instance, we took part in beheading, scalding and plucking feathers from chickens. At other times we assisted in feeding the chickens and collecting their eggs. On more than one occasion, some of the kids got into egg fights. On those days, the chickens apparently didn't lay as many eggs as normal. I remember one chicken that escaped after his head had been removed. It ran under the chicken house, and no one could retrieve it. I'm not sure of the outcome, but I doubt that it made it into the cooking pot.

I hung around a lot with my brother Bobby as we explored the countryside. We walked all over the woods on the Norris horse farm as well as the area around the "spooky" house near National Farm School. It was just an abandoned house, but by the time Tabor kids made up gory stories about it, it was pretty scary just getting close to the place.

Some of my more pleasant memories were picking cherries from the trees bordering the baseball diamond, playing baseball with Sister Viola pitching, climbing pine trees on the front lawn and swimming in the Neshaminy Creek at the "rocks." I recall a Tabor kid falling off a ledge at the "rocks" and a female counselor jumping in to rescue him. On the way in, she scraped herself pretty badly, but I guess she just felt it was all in a day's work.

There were certainly some downsides to living at Tabor. Any vandalism in the general area was blamed on us. It was clearly not a democracy, and there was no such thing as being innocent until proven guilty. I remember the time that Sister Viola slipped on an orange peel that someone had left on the staircase and she ended up falling down the steps. We were all lined up and Sister Wilma gave us a smack on the legs with her cane, because nobody would confess that they had discarded the peel. Tabor kids learned to fake crying as quickly as possible.

Sometimes, of course, we were guilty and were caught in the act. One day I was quarantined on the third floor of the boys' house with whooping cough. I discovered a ball with a small slit in it. I filled it with water and squirted it out the window at kids on the ground floor, getting them wet. I paid for my bad judgment in that case. Another time I sneaked out after dark with my brother and went for a midnight swim in the pool. What great fun to fool the people in charge! There was no price to pay for that adventure. Another time I rode the dumbwaiter down to the storeroom and opened the lock from the inside so my colleagues-in-crime could get some extracurricular snacks.

One of the values I learned at an early age at the Home was never to squeal on a buddy if you get caught violating the rules. Take full responsibility for your actions. Another thing I learned from Lynford Disque, who was always in trouble for one thing or another, was that bribing sometimes works. When he had done something naughty and was about to get punished, he would catch some frogs and present them to Sister Viola, who loved frog legs. She couldn't stay angry at Limpy long, after receiving such a thoughtful gift.

There was camaraderie among Tabor kids that was heartwarming. I remember being sent to bed with no supper for some rule I broke. After the evening meal was complete, a large number of kids had smuggled bits of food in their pockets and delivered it to me in bed. I actually had more to eat that night than I normally would have eaten for supper. That's what friends are for!

The one thing I really hated at Tabor was riding in the school bus with bars on the windows. It seemed to me that it was a prison bus and everyone was looking at us as though we were inmates. I much preferred to walk to school.

My memory of names is not too good after all these years, but I do remember some of the big guys were the Wright brothers, the Hoppe brothers, as well as Eddie and Richie Knauss. I also remember Joey Oxinio and his sister. When my mother remarried and reclaimed the family back, I recall that I was glad to leave, but I did miss the kids.

Jim Kniese joined his three older siblings at Tabor Home in 1944 at the age of 5. He left in 1949 along with Catherine, Charles and Bobby. Jim, who recently lost his wife of 39 years, is a grandfather and presently lives in Pipersville, Pa.

Chapter Four - The 1950s

CHRISTMAS - A TIME FOR REMINISCENCE
By Sister Wilma Loehrig

(This memory is a composite of letters written by Sister Wilma. All of the words are hers, but were edited for this publication.)

The surprise snowstorm in March, which etched every branch in trees and shrubs into a winter wonderland, made me suggest to one of the children that we take a ride in the country right after church services. She had been ill most of the week and did not feel up to attending Sunday school. As we drove through different terrain, we drew each other's attention to various spots of special beauty. At the end of the ride, as we approached Tabor Home, the girl said, "Now the most beautiful spot is before us." We slowly came up the drive and drank in the natural beauty of the Home. We all readily admit that we have external beauty at Tabor, but to those of us who have served here, the real attraction is the need that children present to us in so many intangible ways.

It was in the summer of 1942 that, with reluctance, I accepted the call to become the administrator of Tabor Home. Forces had been at work for sometime to make the offer attractive. I was working in the Reading Inner Mission Society, a referral agency. It was the duty of the staff to visit hospitals and other institutions and seek out those of our own faith and ascertain whether all the services they required were being given to them. We also visited in private homes.

Although my superiors told me they were very satisfied with my work, and the pastors on the territory were grateful and cooperative in planning for the needy ones in their flock, a restless spirit was at work within me. I expressed some of my concerns to our Directing Sister. Sister Anna referred me to a book written by Pearl Buck. I never found out what she must have had in mind when she recommended it, but I discovered something quite different. Miss Buck made the comparison between Oriental and Occidental family life. She made the statement that in the Orient you will find little or no neurosis. She attributed this to family structure. In China, the home is patriarchal. If pressure arises in one place, the children wander to another part of the household and are spared the stress. In America, the family unit is small. Frequently both parents exert heavy pressure on their children to excel. Somewhere along life's pathway a reaction will take place and society will experience neurotic behavior from individuals that have been pushed too hard. All of this made sense to me and instead of rebelling against group care, I became convinced that, for a child who had suffered social shipwreck, this type of placement could be beneficial.

It was with this thinking and feeling that I accepted the call to come to Tabor Home.

How could we give so many children the love and nurture I had growing up with super parents and loving sisters and brothers? Furthermore, I had to be converted to institutional care, and the children of Tabor converted me. I had been a housemother in the girls' dorm for three years in the early 1930s. When I returned eight years later, the same fears surfaced.

The children asked if they could give a party. With permission granted, they were busy all afternoon getting ready. They pooled their meager finances to buy special food. The reception committee led us to our places. Then their performance began and we were filled with songs, dances and recitations. When these ended, we were told that the refreshments were for us. They refused to partake. WOW! In each napkin was a new penny. This need for approval was so poignant that tears welled up within me. The penny was placed in a special box as a reminder of the necessity placed upon us that evening.

Some of the children, who had been in care when I served as a housemother, came to call upon me. I remember asking one of them how it felt to leave home and come into a group setting. His reply was, "Wonderful! The man with the stick couldn't reach me anymore; there were three square meals each day and plenty of kids with whom to have fun. When we get together and talk about Tabor, we all agree that it was the best time of our lives."

World War II was in progress. Some of our good neighbors were spiriting our staff away. First the cook left us and later the laundress. Additional work was placed upon us by rationing food, clothing and gasoline. Our auditorium became the center for community meetings and school children's parties.

The local squire, a friend of Tabor's, decided we needed an American flag for our stage. He solicited the local veterans' organization to donate an appropriate flag and then he planned a formal presentation by the highest-ranking armed forces dignitaries in the community. The ceremony was scheduled for a Sunday afternoon.

The day before the big event, we scrubbed, dusted and waxed every inch of the three buildings. We were dead tired when we went to bed. About half past 10 that evening, someone discovered a broken hot water pipe on the second floor of the girls' dorm. We were all alerted and raced to the rescue. The boys came over from their house and some of the older ones helped to locate the cutoff while the rest of them went upstairs to help get rid of the water. It had found its way through openings to the dining room and even down into the auditorium. The whole place was a mess. But you should have seen the sight that met my eyes, children in goulashes and topcoats using corn and push brooms and mops, working in precision to get rid of the water as quickly as possible. Such teamwork and dedication call forth our praise and admiration. By the time the dignitaries showed up, all the damage had been taken care of.

We knew if we wanted to feed our children well during the war, we had to get busy and preserve fruits and vegetables. We had never done this type of work before, but where there's a will there's a way. Our whole family was pressed into service. Freezing of food was an unknown art at that time. Cold-water packing was the method in use. The term "cold water" is a misnomer. We all felt we were getting a Turkish bath. One girl, who grew up in that era, said she learned so many skills that, after she got married, she put them all to good use and assisted her husband to get his Bachelor of Science degree.

We served as air raid wardens, chaperons at parties, and worked for the P.T.A. Some of the staff were advisors in church youth organizations. When the war was over, we attended a community Thanksgiving service. The pastor was preaching on the war and the many hardships many people had to bear. He said we really hadn't done anything.

After having served as a housemother at Tabor in the mid-30s, I became a student at Temple University. One day as I came down the step at Conwell Hall, I ran into a Tabor Home boy. I asked him what he was doing in the city and he replied that he had just enlisted in the Navy. He had always expressed an interest in higher education and now he was leaving high school without attempting to reach his goal. I reminded him of his earlier intentions. He answered, "How can I go to college?"

At that time there were quite a few immigrants who were attending Temple on scholarships. At that moment, it seemed to me such a pity that our own citizens should be overlooked. I never forgot that encounter and also the fact that there were scholarships available to those who would go after them.

After my return to Tabor, I kept alert to murmurs of improvement among the children as well as higher aspirations. To most of the children, a job meant money in the pocket, freedom and, of course, a car. But, once they got involved in work, they found little or no challenge in this kind of employment. It was not until I had been here for several years that a boy expressed definite interest in education beyond high school. He had a classmate, another Tabor boy, with a similar Intelligence Quotient but without any interest in education beyond high school. I am happy to report that the second boy subsequently did an about-face and picked up his degree and is now a successful teacher.

Not all children whom we inspired to attain higher goals remained with us until they graduated from high school. Quite a few have returned to thank us for opening new horizons to them. They stayed with their dreams until they were realized. And now they are enjoying satisfying work and have gained status among their fellowman. Many have returned to the place where they prepared themselves for the next day's recitation. We called it study hall. They all confessed they had not been as diligent as they should have been. However, that spot had planted a seed that said, in effect, "If you want something out of life, you have to come prepared." I am quite sure that there are few schoolteachers who realize how much work had gone into those hours on the part of staff.

The war years robbed us of manpower. The lawns became shaggy looking. In the orchard and in back of the boys' dorm, the grass grew too quickly for us. One of the Sisters (Viola) loved sheep, and one of her bargaining points was that lambs could serve as our lawn mowers. After listening to her suggestion for an entire year, I asked her one spring day if she wanted to go for a ride. She did not know our destination but it was Rice's sale. It was the first time that either of us had been to an auction. The auctioneer kept us spellbound. He was aware of our presence and quite amused at our naive behavior. We had looked at the lambs to be auctioned and set our hearts on two beauties. The auctioneer had a man planted among the bidders to up prices. This man began to raise the price of the two lambs. The people in the crowd refused to bid. Finally, one man turned to the shill and said, "Don't you know they want them? Stop your bidding."

Now that we purchased them, how should we get them home? We were not leaving without them. We couldn't handle them ourselves so we asked a man to place them in our passenger car. Sister Viola drove, and I held them in the back seat. By the time we arrived home, the grade school children were returning from school. We put dog collars on them and tied them to the clothesline. The children made a semicircle around them and loved and admired them from the start.

Making pets of them was a mistake. Before fall arrived, they had taken control. It was difficult to confine them. One fine day they took another ride. Weeks grew into months before Sister Viola ate one morsel of meat. She would not be guilty of eating her darlings.

Pets have always been part of the children's lives. Parents brought in chicks and ducklings each Easter. The children admired them until the end of the day, when they found their way into the pantry of the admin building. It usually became my job to see that they stayed alive. The ducklings became ganders that chased everyone who came into contact with them. The chicks grew into lovely white roosters. The concern of infection that poultry may carry finally wiped out this practice.

Two incidents have etched themselves into my memory. One occurred on Memorial Day. The local community had a parade and a memorial service at the gravesite of veterans. One of our younger boys wanted to know if he had to attend the parade. He was told that he did not have to go if he didn't want to. Half an hour later, marching feet were heard outside the admin building. We went to the window to see what was going on. Here was this boy in the lead, carrying an American flag, while the rest had empty #10 tin cans or mouthpiece instruments. They were producing the sounds of fifes and drums. They marched around the buildings and then headed for the woods where their pets were buried, and fired cap gun salutes over each grave. The "soldiers" then solemnly retreated to the boys' dorm. For them the ceremony had a lot of meaning. We, as observers, felt it was done in a very dignified manner.

Two chicks that grew up into roosters met their demise sometime in the summer. We all felt bad about it. As December approached, one of the boys asked what kind of roosters I would like to have. I told him that would depend upon what kind of chickens we had. He wasn't satisfied with my answer. He came back with the same question several times and each time he got the same reply. He finally gave up. On Christmas Eve we normally celebrated our family party. When the time came to distribute the gifts, he asked if he could help. We had invited the Pastor Repass and his wife to join us. They were a childless couple and to them a large family was an enigma. They were certainly not prepared to cope with all the commotion that was going on. The boy got up and brought a large carton to me. As I opened the flaps, two of the most beautiful leghorn roosters I had ever seen rose straight up toward the lights. They flew past Mrs. Repass's face and then raced around the dining room. We all gave chase. When we finally captured them, I took them to the accustomed place, the pantry in the admin building. Tears of joy and appreciation flowed down my cheeks. I knew it had taken much thought and quite a few weeks of spending money of three boys to purchase these lovely creatures. When I returned to the dining room, Mrs. Repass had not recovered from the shock.

In order to have food to preserve, we had to grow it. Although my family always lived in the suburbs, we always had a vegetable garden. So, I grew up with the knowledge of varieties and culture of growing things. With this background and a special effort to remember the kinds and varieties of seeds we had gotten that year, I went into a board of trustee's meeting. As usual, the farm came into discussion. The only thing that had been left to the farmer to purchase was the seed potatoes. And what do you know, the only question the men asked was, "Sister, what kind of potatoes did you plant?" I glanced around the room to size up the farming knowledge of the board members. I concluded they were all city-bred and knew nothing of potatoes. I replied, "White potatoes, of course." The peals of laughter that went up were disconcerting.

Later, I approached the farmer and asked him the name of the variety. He looked at me and said, "It's a new strain and I can't remember the name." That fall, one of the directors looked at me slyly and said, "Sister, what kind of potatoes did you end up planting?"

People (mostly Taborites) have asked me over the years to write a Tabor story. I once wrote a brief and sent it to several of them. Carl Hoppe replied, "The reading triggered a mental camera and tape recorder, which flashed upon the inward eye and often remembered, but seldom verbalized, childhood. Each of us who have acted a part has felt many times that here was a story worth telling. Though it may be doubtful as to whether the Tabor story

123

would achieve Book-of-the-Month status, to those who have lived the story, there is no doubt as to its status in their lives."

Mary Ralston Wood wrote, "I was thinking about Tabor Home at Christmas tonight (1980). It is like a storybook novel. I don't think anybody could comprehend it or visualize the happiness and normal childhood that was planted in our minds. I thank the Lord for the privilege of being one of the Tabor Home kids. I have been able to meet people and the world has treated me very good. I have a good husband, two lovely girls, two beautiful grandchildren, a nice job (supervisor-surgery), coming in contact with all classes of people, and knowing how to handle situations at the right time."

Captain Wilbur Wright, U.S. Air Force, wrote, "I am very thankful that my formative years were spent at Tabor because I learned many lessons that are priceless. The associations that I had with you, your wonderful staff and the very fine group of boys and girls at Tabor during those 12 years gave me a background of hard work, fair play, and an awareness that I was indeed a very fortunate person to have grown up in a happy, healthy environment. It taught me to be proud of my accomplishments and to be compassionate to the less fortunate. I'm sure that these lessons just 'rubbed off' on me but I think that had I grown up under a different set of circumstances, perhaps these lessons would not have come so swiftly."

Sara Duckworth Carlson wrote, "Thank God there was a Tabor Home when I was a youngster. I definitely feel my life would have been totally different today and my outlook on life could have been far less enjoyable. We got a good regimen of work, sleep, balanced diet and play. Tabor Home taught me how to handle all situations and get along with many different personalities. Today my home is run smoothly and the security I feel in my adult life is ever present and felt by my children and those around me. This is a direct result of the love, security, and religion taught and conveyed by all who worked and managed Tabor Home."

Commander Orville Wright, U.S. Navy, wrote, "I also think there is a great deal of truth in Jake Highton's analysis of living at Tabor. In addition to a strong work ethic and development of interpersonal skills, it gave one a self-reliance that would be hard to duplicate in a family environment. I am not sure I would go so far as to advocate institutional living for everyone, but the benefits (a strong sense of loyalty and teamwork, a clear definition of morality, and an insight into self-introspection) were invaluable. I have said on many occasions that, after spending 27 years in a military environment, I would be most comfortable with Tabor kids if I had a military mission to accomplish. They are mission-oriented, competitive, and they put the group ahead of self. I have personally been very fortunate in life with a series of successes both in the military and in business with IBM. My children are all married and successful, and I could not be happier with my present situation. As an example, I was just given an achievement award by IBM. I plan to move to England in 1995 for about three years where I will be in charge of flight-testing British helicopters. IBM won the competition as system prime contractor over an English defense company." (Note: IBM laid off 20,000 people in 1991 - Sister Wilma)

This is a sampling of what you have helped to accomplish. As Carl and Wilbur said, many have not written such concise analyses, but they have expressed themselves in greetings. They keep us informed about themselves, their families, their faith in God, and their participation in the church of which they are members.

Time is of the essence right now so I will have to end it here. I could tell you more about the farm, parties among and for the children, incidents that happened while we were getting ready for open house, plays put on for our family by our family (especially the one where the children impersonated the staff members), plays put on for the public, trips, isolation, graduation from high school and college, and courtships and marriage.

One question that always startles me is, "What do you know?" It reminds me of a staff member asking one of the boys, "What did you do?" The boy sat down and had a real mental catharsis by reciting to him all the misdemeanors he could pack into a half hour's time.

Well, life has been so rich and full that more than one volume could be written in response to, "What do you know?" It has been a wonderful experience!

Thank you, God, for an abundant life. Thank you, my friends, for your help. Blessed Christmas, Sister Wilma

---

Sister Wilma Loehrig relieved Sister Lena Beideck as the head Lutheran deaconess at Tabor Home for Children in 1942. In the early '30s she had been a housemother in the girls' dorm. She was born in Reading, Pa., in 1906 into a family of nine children. Sister Wilma retired in 1969 after serving more than 32 years at Tabor. She died in 1995 at the age of 89.

BEST TIME OF MY LIFE
By John (Jack) Freas

My background was rather unusual, even by Tabor Home standards. I was the ninth child in a family of 12 children. My parents separated in the early 1940s, and the children were farmed out to different homes, some private and others institutional. The five youngest were sent to a Lutheran home in Montgomery County called River Crest Home. I was 5 or 6 years old at the time. Two of my siblings went to live with my grandparents, and two other sisters ended up in a girls' home in Germantown.

About two years later my younger brother Walt and I were put in a foster home. Life seemed reasonably normal to me, but evidently my "high spirits" were more than my foster parents could handle. They "gave me back" in 1950, electing to keep Walt as an only child. This decision came as a complete shock to me, but as a 10-year-old transient I was accustomed to change. Tabor Home was to be my address for the next nine years.

Having lived in a Lutheran home before, the change in setting did not frighten or terrify me, but I was taken aback by the large number of beds (23) in the front room. This was my first experience in dormitory living. I did have real fear that I might never see my parents again. How could I know that the courts would keep them apprised of my location and status?

One of the nice things about being raised at Tabor was there were always guys and girls with similar values and interests. I remember hanging around with Rudy Gold, Jim Jeffries, Joe Oxinio, Clyde and Harry Beagle, Marian Tacker and Kay Welch. Joe and Kay were classmates, and we all graduated together in 1959.

The memories I have of Tabor are mostly positive. I clearly remember how much fun it was on May Day. And killing, scalding and plucking chickens will remain in my mind's eye forever. It seems that Sister Wilma always had a dog or two. I distinctly recall a German Shepherd named Fritz that bit me one Sunday, because he thought I was trying to take his bone away. I was completely innocent, and my father, who was visiting me at the time, was furious that I was bitten. I just considered it part of the game.

Mandatory study halls in the admin building were enjoyable, and I maintained a solid C average throughout high school. My transition from elementary school at Edison to high school at Central Bucks was relatively smooth. I really enjoyed playing sports at CB, particularly football, where I played offensive center and defensive middle linebacker.

I liked all phases of football and would often practice kicking field goals even though I was not the designated kicker. It paid off during a game against Lansdale, because I was called upon to attempt a field goal and was successful. It was all the more noteworthy to me, because my younger sister, who attended Lansdale, was in the stands and saw it. By the way, we won the game! My last two years were quite successful on the gridiron with only two losses against eight wins each year.

My relationship with Sister Wilma was quite good, although as I got older we had our differences. I believed her absolute control of who left the grounds was a little "over the top." I dislocated my shoulder during a high school football game and had to have my jersey cut away at the hospital for treatment. I went back to the school and attended the sock hop before returning home. Sister Wilma greeted me with a royal "chewing out," because I had not called and let her know the status of my injury. That was the first time I realized that she had been listening to every football game on the radio and was very concerned when she heard about my hospitalization. I gained new respect for her from that incident.

The barn duties were shared among four of the older boys in the late 1950s. Because Joe Oxinio and I were playing varsity football, we would milk the cows and muck the stalls in the morning before school, and two other boys (Rudy Gold and Jimmy Jeffries) would handle farm duties in the afternoon. It worked out well, and Harry (Boog) Burmiester, the farmer-in-charge, seemed satisfied.

If asked to characterize my overall feelings about being raised at Tabor Home, I would say it was the best time in my life. It kept me on the straight and narrow, and gave me a sense of responsibility at a young age. Surprisingly, life on the farm prepared me for life. I joined the Marine Corps after graduating from high school, and boot camp wasn't that hard. It's as if Tabor was a training ground for the Marines.

I won't be a Pollyanna and tell you living at Tabor was perfect. In high school I remember being embarrassed by being from the Home. It probably held me back somewhat in life, because I didn't have sufficiently high aspirations and goals.

Despite the fact that my parents separated and broke up our family, both my father and mother supported me throughout my time at the Home. My relationship with them both has always been quite positive. Although my siblings were dispersed in childhood, we maintain contact as adults and we get along very well.

After four years in the Marine Corps, I got a job with Philadelphia Electric and worked for there for 31 years. All in all, I am pleased to have been raised at Tabor Home, because it gave me a good set of values, valuable training and habits that have lasted a lifetime.

John Freas spent nine years at Tabor Home arriving in 1950. He is retired, the father of three children with his first wife, and presently lives in Philadelphia with his second wife Bernice.

I WASN'T A SPECIAL LITTLE ANGEL
By Ginny Hirschbuhl Carson

My story begins in 1948 when, as a 3-year-old, I was enrolled at Tabor Home along with my sister Carol, who was seven years older. My four remaining siblings were farmed out to relatives. Our family, living in Lacy Park, Pa., (near Willow Grove) had fallen apart, and our parents essentially abandoned us. My rather unstable mother was unable to cope with the care and feeding of six children.

At that age I was not prepared to live in an institution, no matter how well equipped it was to deal with children from dysfunctional families. And Tabor Home was not. My first memories were being scared to death and hiding under tables to avoid being seen. I was assigned to the "baby" room along with two other 3- or 4-year-old girls.

Today I would probably have been diagnosed as having attention deficit disorder (ADD), an affliction that was not recognized in the late 1940s. Instead I was branded as unruly, and duly disciplined. I spent many hours in isolation because of my spirited personality and dislike of authority.

I remember Sisters Emma and Jenny, who supervised in the girls' dormitory, as being sweet and kind, but I cannot say the same about Sister Wilma, the head administrator. I was always fearful of her and considered her cold and rather evil. There is some irony that my sister Carol was one of her favorites. I observed her behavior to a number of children and did my best to avoid her.

Although I was never a good student, I was glad when I became old enough to attend the elementary school in Edison, about a half-mile south of Tabor. I thought the teachers like Miss Ruth and Miss Young were great, as well as Mr. Hearn in the sixth grade. I never really felt smart in school, but I appreciated the interest the teachers showed in me.

As a child I was often in trouble, because I possessed a rebellious streak. I could never be described as a "special little angel." For some reason I really despised being controlled, and I felt rules were just guidelines that could be broken as long as you didn't get caught. I would leave the grounds without permission when I wanted, play hooky from school or go night sledding after curfew. In the last example, I was caught by Sister Wilma and her

German Shepherd dog and was confined to my room as a punishment.

Change was always a most difficult process for me, and transitioning from elementary to junior high was especially traumatic. My self-image was one of a tough girl from Tabor Home, but the challenges of higher learning were quite daunting. It didn't help that I considered myself stupid.

I distinctly recall an incident that has haunted me my entire life. I was waiting to be picked up by my family for a short vacation. Sister Wilma saw me and asked me if I knew where Anna Beagle was. When I told her she was up in the woods, she sent me to fetch her. I replied that Anna wouldn't listen to me. I was told not to return without her.

As expected, Anna ignored my directive to report to Sister Wilma now. Fearing that my failure to carry out my mission would result in punishment, I picked up a stick in frustration and hurled it at the obstinate girl.

As bad luck would have it, the stick contained an embedded nail and it struck her in the face. With blood and tears flowing, Anna dashed from the woods seeking first aid.

Punishment came swift and sure. Vacation was cancelled, and I was awarded one week in isolation. The only visitor was Sister Wilma's dog that I was deathly afraid of. Whenever the "killer" would wander into my room, I would hold my breath and pretend to be asleep until he departed. A very traumatic week for me!

Any time my family (older sisters and aunts) would take me away on weekends or for short vacations in the summer, I would hate the thought of having to return to the Home. My relationship with Sister Wilma deteriorated as I got older, and finally she directed me not to return after a summer visit with my mother and stepfather. I had assumed my mother was informed that I was no longer allowed back at Tabor. But when I told her that I couldn't return, the look on her face indicated otherwise. She was not ready to have a 12-year-old rebel invade the one-bedroom apartment she shared with her new husband.

My new environment did not result in stability or normalcy for my teenage years. Between a shortage of food and being constantly behind in rent payments, I thought I'd have been better off staying at Tabor where I was assured of clothes and meals.

Now, in looking back at nine years at the Home, I have mixed feelings. I am thankful, because it kept me alive. I do not think I would have survived otherwise. It developed a self-reliance that was a great benefit later in life. I loved the security and the "happy times," such as Christmas, sing-alongs and campfires. On the other hand, it was distressing that I had so little control of my life. Children had no rights in those days. I am thankful that society has changed for the better regarding that.

Postscript: I dropped out of Abington High School, married at 19 and had three girls. I was way too young and immature for marriage, and it ended in divorce. After a second failed marriage, I went back to school, started therapy and turned my life around. As I approach three-score years, I can honestly say I like who I am, realize I am quite intelligent and am an advocate of disadvantaged children. My girls have all turned out well, and I am very proud of them. So, perhaps, all's well that ends well.

Ginny Hirschbuhl came to Tabor with her older sister Carol in 1948 at the age of 3 and left nine years later. She is the proud mother of three girls and lives in Horsham, Pa.

YOU CAN CALL ME CHARLOTTE McKENZIE
By Cathy Welch Watson

The year was 1946. World War II and rationing were over, and things were starting to return to normal in the country. For the Welch family living in Doylestown, consisting of 5-year-old Kay (me), 3-year-old Peggy and 2-year-old Johnny, adventures in a strange new world were just starting.

Peggy and I were shipped off to Tabor Home after our grandmother died and Mother experienced a nervous breakdown. Close friends living in Chalfont, Pa., adopted Johnny, and Mother checked into a mental hospital to recover. At Tabor children were assigned rooms based upon age, so the Welch sisters were separated upon arrival.

Although the first few weeks and months at Tabor are very hazy, I recall riding the bus to school and taking our meager lunches in a brown bag. It was quite humiliating, because "normal" children owned lunch boxes or bought their lunches at school. I remember hating to ride the Tabor bus.

School was never hard for me, and I always got good grades. Despite being a good student, I was constantly in trouble with the teachers, because I insisted on being the class clown. I would disrupt the class by bringing in water guns or jumping out the window on a dare; you get the picture. My favorite subjects were math, English, history and geography. I disliked physical education and biology.

By the time I was 12 years old, I figured out how to play hooky without getting caught. I remember taking the bus into Philly and watching American Bandstand with Dick Clark. I thought that was really cool and was careful not to get seen on television.

Some other memories of my pre-teen years were having fun with other Tabor kids and playing games like kick the can or hide and seek. On one occasion, I locked myself into an old refrigerator. It was lucky other kids were looking for me or I might not be writing this story.

My sister and I would see our mother on visiting days and would also visit her at Christmas and spend a week together in the summer. Unfortunately, she disappeared from our lives about 1951. I only saw my father one time. He stopped by one Sunday, accompanied by a guard that was transporting him to another prison. I don't know any details about why he was in prison or what happened to him after his incarceration was over.

I am a naturally optimistic person. As I look back at my childhood, most of the memories are positive. I recall mandatory study hall in the administration building from 7 to 9 p.m. each school night. I would quickly complete my homework so I could play scrabble with Sister Wilma. I never figured out why I was one of her favorites. On more than one occasion she would take me to the movies with her. Perhaps she saw my potential and overlooked the fact that I was always in trouble with authority figures.

My final act of rebellion was in the spring of my senior year at Central Bucks High School. I met a boy from Lansdale named Bobby Swope at a football game and became friends with him and his family. Another Tabor girl, Mary Covey, and I planned to run away and get jobs working in Lansdale. While planning the caper, a third girl, Pattie Potter, asked if she could come along. With the help of another Tabor friend, Mary Wilson, I created a map showing the highways leading to Florida and left it under one of the beds. It was Mary's task to ensure someone would find it and show it to the people looking for us.

On the appointed day, Bobby, his older brother and two friends picked up the adventuresome trio. By nightfall, things started going haywire. I had the money to bankroll the escape, but it somehow wound up in the pockets of my partners-in-crime. After I discovered the loss, I recovered my money and told them they were on their own. Without a plan, Mary and Pattie asked to be dropped off back at Tabor, which we did.

The Swope family was good enough to let me bunk at their home until I could get a job and find a room for myself. I called myself Charlotte McKenzie and began a job search. In short order, I found one, but the company required some information including my social security number. Two weeks later I was in my room in the evening when there was a loud knock at the door. When I inquired who was there, a reply came, "The police." After I opened the door, one of the officers asked me my name. I replied, "You can call me Charlotte McKenzie."

"Show me some ID," was his next demand. I quickly confessed and was transported to the police station. My glamorous existence had lasted less than four weeks.

The same evening Sister Wilma drove over to Lansdale and

claimed me. I was restricted from having contact with any of the Tabor kids and was placed under admin house arrest. The only exception was working in the kitchen for Sister Jenny.

Although I had missed a month of school (with final exams looming), the high school principal agreed to let me graduate if I passed the final exams. Fortunately, I did pass them, and in May 1959 I became an alumna of Central Bucks High School. My 13 years at Tabor were over.

After several months living with my brother in Chalfont, I moved back to Lansdale and obtained a job.

Living at Tabor was not all that bad. There were a lot of good times, and I know I was better off than a lot of my friends. Christmas at Tabor was great! So were trips to the circus, as well as baseball and football games. I didn't like mandatory church, but I am still Lutheran.

An interesting postscript: On a weekend vacation to Beachhaven, N.J., I stopped by a drugstore and, much to my surprise, saw my mother behind the counter, working as a clerk. She didn't recognize me, so I introduced myself as her oldest daughter. She had remarried and was living a completely new life. We have spent time together since, and I am quite fond of her.

Life at Tabor gave me an independence that was not very compatible with married life. After multiple marriages, I realized I am better off single. I returned to school, got my certification as an accountant and have supported myself my whole life. I retired several years ago, but am working part-time and really enjoying life.

Cathy is retired, the mother of two daughters and has six grandchildren. She lives in Sacramento, Calif., and is an avid NASCAR fan.

I WAS DEVASTATED WHEN HE DROVE OFF
By Ann Osgood Whiteside

My story begins in late 1951 when, at the age of 14, I arrived at Tabor Home with my 11-year-old twin siblings (Fred and Patricia) and 4-year-old Tom. As the oldest child in a rather normal family, I had mastered the necessary homemaking skills to fill in as a junior mother. My mother had left us, and my dad was recuperating from a bout with malaria and was unemployed. We lived in the Hatboro area for a short period of time, but it was obvious that a more permanent solution had to be found.

The Osgood children spent the summer of 1951 in a foster home. In October our father drove us to Tabor and deposited us into the hands of Miss Evelyn and Sister Wilma, who scared the daylights out of me. My next memory was the devastation I felt as my father drove off. It almost felt as though it was not really happening and I would wake up from this nightmare. Unfortunately, Tabor was reality, and we were on our own.

I can't relate to a child who is institutionalized at a very young age and knows no other existence, but I know what it is like to change from a family environment to a children's home. It was frightening beyond belief. Even though I was initially concerned about my siblings' welfare, I quickly got caught up in my own dilemma and decided to let them fend for themselves.

I think the most terrifying aspect of my experience was coping with girls that had come from tough sections of Philadelphia and were accustomed to intimidating others with threats of physical violence. Two such colleagues were Patsy and a girl named Lorraine. I really feared for my well-being.

On the flip side, there were also very sweet and considerate girls that would go out of their way to help and befriend new girls. I especially remember Bette Simon and Doris Gold as special friends.

We lived quite a structured life at the Home. The Lutheran deaconesses were assigned as housemothers and supervisors. Sister Emma was in charge of the girls' dormitory and ran a taut ship, but I remember her as a taciturn busybody whose method of operation resembled that of a snoopy private detective. Sister Jenny was charged with feeding the 80 children in the Home, and many of my chores were kitchen-related. I recall making lunches by lining up rows of bread in assembly-line fashion and slapping on the bologna or peanut butter and jelly or whatever was the sandwich-of-the-day. Another chore that is seared in my mind is polishing the wooden floors in the huge dining room.

Not all of my memories are grim. We had fun riding on the dumb-waiter that connected the kitchen with the basement storeroom. Of course, we were not permitted to ride in it, but the opportunity was too inviting. Smoking cigarettes on the fire escape was another forbidden act to which I also succumbed.

My first three years in high school were not happy, carefree years. I didn't adjust well to such dramatic changes in my life. Our father saw us during visiting hours on Sunday, but we never developed a close relationship with him. I did not see my mother until some years after I left Tabor. My life seemed to be in constant state of turmoil with no one available to discuss my concerns and problems. The housemothers were not trained to deal with troubled youths and would have been overwhelmed with the high ratio of children to available counselors.

During the summer following my junior year at Central Bucks High School, I ended up with a full-time job as a nanny for a 3-year-old son of Marylee Lawrey, daughter of Dr. McKinney, president of the Tabor Home board of directors. It isn't that I hated the job or that I wasn't qualified for the assignment. My objection was that I didn't have a say in the decision. For someone who had difficulty with change, this incident has irritated me for the past 50 years. It would have been so simple to ask me if I was willing to change schools my senior year and take on this assignment. I might not have agreed to it, but any book on leadership would stress the advantages of signing up volunteers versus using the draft.

After six months as the primary caregiver for a 3-year-old, I was assigned an additional duty to look after newborn twins. For an 18-year-old girl in her senior year of high school, this was a disheartening blow. I went to school, cooked all the meals and minded children in my "free" time. They lived in the country, and I had zero social life. I was not a happy camper. By the way, there was no stipend of any kind other than room and board. The Lawreys were lovely people so life was bearable, but I was happy to finally get on with life after graduation.

My upbringing at Tabor certainly shaped my life. I developed into a very independent woman, and I do not allow anyone to take advantage of me. For that I am proud.

There is a happy ending to my story. I spent my life in the banking industry, met and married a wonderful man and raised two children that I am extremely proud of.

Ann Osgood came to Tabor when she was 14 years old and remained there until graduation in 1955. She is the mother of two children and lives in Harleysville, Pa., with her husband Joe Whiteside.

IT WAS A GREAT LIFE-LEARNING EXPERIENCE
By Joan Bach Youells

The Bachs were just a normal, middle-class family living in Neshaminy Valley, Pa. I was the oldest child and my brother Frank was four years younger. In 1949 my parents decided to separate, and our mother became the head of the household. After Mom got a second-shift job, it became obvious that we could not continue as a family unit with the responsibility of a 6-year-old being placed in my lap. She decided to send us to Tabor Home for Children in 1951.

Although the Home was only a few miles away in distance, it was light years away in similarity. Anyone coming from a "normal" home is initially struck by the size of the operation. It was surprising to see large numbers of people doing every-day tasks at the same time, such as 80 children sitting down to a meal simultaneously.

My first reaction was fear of the unknown, but I had lived with other relatives and was fairly adept at adjusting to their house rules. In fact, I had attended nine schools in seven years. So even though coming to Tabor was a huge event in my life, my quiet demeanor and adaptability prepared me for the scary, yet exciting future. I was concerned about the welfare of 6-year-old Frank, who was living apart from me in the boys' dormitory. But I got to see him at mealtime, and he seemed to be taking the setback in stride. In just a few weeks, living at Tabor seemed quite normal to me.

One of the best aspects of living in a children's home is that you come in contact with a lot of kids with similar backgrounds and interests. Many of them turn into life-long friends. Somehow, even though you may not see them for years, the intervening time melts away and common experiences are re-lived and the bond of childhood is tightened once more. I feel this way about many of the girls who were at Tabor in the early 1950s such as Pattie Potter, Marian Tacker, Kay Welch, Jean Wilson and Patsy Osgood.

Unlike some of the other kids, I really enjoyed living at Tabor. I liked working in the kitchen with Sister Jenny and learning cooking skills like making scrapple. Even things that grossed out other girls, like killing chickens and plucking their feathers, didn't affect me at all. I enjoyed eating the chicken, even though I assisted in the entire butchering process.

Tabor had a fairly rigid set of rules, and discipline was

delivered rapidly and often publicly. I clearly remember being quite disturbed when Sister Wilma gave Doris Gold a slap across the face for something she said at dinner. Doris was someone I always admired and looked up to, so to see her humiliated before all the kids in the dining room was very upsetting. I tended to follow the rules and almost never experienced the wrath of the supervising Sisters.

My thoughts about elementary school were that I studied as much as was necessary to pass each grade. After sixth grade we all went to junior high in Doylestown. I remember that pot smoking was common among the students, but I chose not to participate.

Both my parents were quite supportive during my years in the Home, and they visited on alternate Sundays quite religiously. In that regard, Frank and I were luckier than some of the other children who saw their parents only on special occasions.

While I was in the ninth grade, Sister Emma died unexpectedly. Almost all the girls were quite upset. One evening, after a particularly trying day, Sister Wilma stated that the girls' poor behavior had contributed to Sister Emma's death. I blurted out that Sister Emma was quite critical of the way you (Sister Wilma) ran the home and that caused her death. As you might imagine, my remark escalated into a huge verbal fight. That incident marked a milestone in my road toward self-confidence.

I subsequently ran away from Tabor to my mother's house and told her I was not going back. She agreed, and both Frank and I left the Home that week.

Looking back, spending five years at Tabor was a life-learning experience and I have no regrets about the time I spent there. I made many good friends, had both good and sad times, and enjoyed being part of a big family.

I graduated from William Tennant High School in 1959 and immediately got a job. I married William Youells in 1964. I feel very fortunate that my life has turned out the way it did and would not give up my years at Tabor for anything. Over the years I have tried to instill in my children the value of family in the big scheme of things. It is of premier importance.

Joan Bach came to Tabor with her brother Frank in 1951 at the age of 10 and left five years later. Her husband of 36 years died in 2000. She is the proud mother of three adult children and lives in Upper Black Eddy, Pa.

THE ONLY THING I HATED
WAS THE COD LIVER OIL
By David Malyn, Ph.D.

My father deserted my mother shortly after I was born. There were no social support systems then, and being a single mother was quite difficult. I was cared for by a number of relatives, because my mother was working full-time. After a few years, though, the combination of her full-time employment and my hyperactivity led to my being placed in Tabor Home.

A Lutheran sister, or deaconess, ran the home. Her name was Sister Wilma. Another deaconess named Sister Edith was in charge of the boys' house. The Sisters were very strict and expected all the children to toe the line. I would estimate that about 40 boys and 40 girls lived at Tabor Home when I was there. They ranged in age from about 6 to about 18.

I came to Tabor Home before I started third grade. Up until that time, I had lived with my mother in an apartment. When I came to Tabor, I had to adjust to the change from having my own room to sleeping in a large room with 23 other boys. One of the factors that sticks out in my mind when I think of Tabor is the physical setting. I have lived in many places in the United States and have visited a number of foreign countries, but I have never been to a place that is as beautiful as rural Pennsylvania. Living on a farm in a rural setting offers many advantages to a child, although some, like pulling weeds in a field or picking up potatoes, did not seem like advantages at the time. We learned the lessons of hard work and responsibility. Each child had daily and weekly jobs to do. The older boys worked on the farm and younger ones had clean-up duties around the boys' house. Being assigned a job working on the farm was a rite of passage for a boy at Tabor Home. Only the big kids worked on the farm.

We went to bed early and got up early, and children did their jobs before breakfast. Much of the food we ate was home-grown on the farm. I remember fishing in a stream behind the barn, and a lot of swimming all summer long. I also remember many homemade apple pies. One not so pleasant memory was lining up for a spoon of cod liver oil after dinner. I can't think of anything that I have ever had in my life that tastes worse than cod liver oil.

We attended the public school in Doylestown. The town's people or those we came in contact with at school did not always hold Tabor kids in the highest regard. One afternoon, as a group of us walked home after school, one of the boys stole a candy bar at a local store and was caught by the proprietor. No one else was involved and, in fact, we were angry with the kid for getting us in trouble. Of course, we were all indicted when the owner despairingly stated in a loud voice, "What can you expect from Tabor Home kids?"

Every Sunday we rode on the bus to St. Paul's Lutheran Church in downtown Doylestown. We also attended many activities at St. Paul's, such as Vacation Bible School and Christmas programs. Our religious training did not just consist of going to church on Sunday. We sang a hymn and said a prayer before every meal and prayed as a group before going to bed at night.

On Christmas we had a lot of parties given to us by various local groups. My favorite was a father-son party given by the men of a church group. They would come and pick up all the boys and take us to their church for a night of games and food. I have many fond memories of Tabor Home and am very grateful that such a place existed at the time when I was a child.

Post Script: As a school psychologist I deal with many children from dysfunctional families who have a multitude of problems. I have several times seen a child removed from such a home, placed in foster care, returned to his dysfunctional family, removed a second time, placed in a different foster home and then returned again to his family. I often think how much better it would be for these children if a place like Tabor Home was an available option. I was far better off at Tabor, because after I left I lived with my mother and an abusive stepfather for six months. Then I went to my father and his family who did not want me. That situation lasted until I graduated from high school. I wish I had been able to stay at Tabor Home until I became an adult. Living at Tabor Home was probably the best thing that happened to me in my youth.

David Malyn lived at Tabor Home from 1955 until 1961, arriving there when he was 8 years old. He is married with two children and is a school psychologist in Salt Lake City, Utah.

ONE GREAT BIG HAPPY FAMILY
By Lillian Brown Clough

Although I came to Tabor in 1943 at age 3, I really don't remember anything about those first several years. My first memory was going to kindergarten in the study hall in the admin building. I liked school and it seemed like fun at the time. That love for school transferred into elementary school for a while. I distinctly remember my second grade teacher, Mrs. Ruth. She had a very positive influence on my life. My love affair with school came to an end in the sixth grade when I found out that recess was cancelled. I decided that two could play that game. I wouldn't do any more homework. Such reasoning did not make me a favorite among teachers or Sister Wilma.

The reason my brother Dick (age 9) and I ended up in the Home in the first place was that my father died right after my birth, and my mother was simply not capable of raising three small children by herself. This was before the days of social welfare that could assist single mothers in keeping their families intact. She did manage to get my 6-year-old brother Herb into Girard College. Several years later she enrolled Dick into Milton Hershey Industrial College, so I remained the sole Brown at Tabor.

My mother lived in Doylestown near the high school, and she would visit me every third week or so, rotating among all the siblings. Of course, when I enrolled in junior high and high school, I visited with her a lot more.

Growing up under ideal circumstances is not an easy journey. For a girl in a children's home, it is full of sadness, disappointments and frustrating events. That is not to say there weren't fun times, because there were plenty. But the knowledge that you did not have the support of parents was always in the back of your mind. And there was no one around to remind you that you were someone "special" and could be whatever you wanted to be.

By the time I got to sixth grade, Edison had changed from one through eight grades to one through six. We all were bussed to Central Bucks for seventh grade. I remember that the transition was quite difficult for me. Tabor kids were generally looked down on (or at least that was my perception), and my academic performance was marginal at best.

My memories of Tabor are mostly positive. I loved hanging around with all the kids, sharing their clothes and experiences. I was quite close to Sister Emma, and I remember crying when I heard she had died. Living at Tabor taught me a lot of home-making skills, which helped me a lot in adulthood. I never felt that I wanted for anything, and most of the time we were just one great big happy family. Going to Cape May in the summer or to the Ice Capades in the winter were just some of the adventures that Tabor kids got to participate in.

Of course there were injustices to deal with. In high school I put on a few extra pounds and was accused of shaming the Home by becoming pregnant. It wasn't even close to the truth, but the accusation hurt for a long time. Another time my mother signed up to assist on May Day but failed to show, because my brother caught the measles and she had to care for him. This event put her in the doghouse with Sister Wilma, and it was no easy task to escape once you were sentenced.

One last thought on my last few years at the Home. I volunteered to babysit on weekends and in the summer for several of Dr. McKinney's children. I was treated very well and really enjoyed myself. One of my playmates was the daughter of Tom Cahill, who later was elected governor of New Jersey, so that was the type of company I kept. I looked forward to taking the train to Wayne Junction on Friday and returning on Sunday. It was a real adventure for me.

Even though I would move heaven and earth to avoid sending my child to any children's home, I am pleased with the training and experiences that came my way. I felt capable of fending for myself. It made me independent and gave me a feeling of competence in facing the world's challenges after I graduated high school and was essentially on my own.

Lillian Brown came to Tabor Home at the age of 3 with her older brother Dick. She left after graduating from Central Bucks High School in 1958. She lives in Doylestown, and is the mother of two adult sons.

I REALIZED I WAS MUCH BETTER OFF THAN ALICE
By Pattie Potter McKelvey

To a happy 4-year-old, life is a series of new experiences, constant wonderment, insecurities, joy of familiar routines and a need to be loved. My life turned upside down in 1946. The trauma I endured when a social worker physically removed me from my mother and escorted me to Tabor Home still remains, after nearly 60 years. I was scared and crying at this unknown turn of events, but I recovered quickly and made the best of my situation. Upon reflection, I believe my father had a drinking problem and my mother was unable to cope under the circumstances. My siblings were shipped off to foster care and I, alone, faced institutional living for the next 14 years.

Friends tell me I was an extroverted, blond-headed, pretty child that made friends quickly. Many of the older boys treated me as a younger sister, which included a fair amount of teasing, but any attention is attention to a young child, and I relished it. Even Sister Wilma, who did her best to avoid favorites, seemed to treat me as a "pet" over the years. I did my best to follow the rules, and seldom got into trouble, which helped.

As I think back on my life at the Home, most memories are happy and positive. Easter and Christmas were especially joyful times. Presents were really a big deal at Tabor, and we certainly got our share in December each year. Even an individual box containing an orange, nuts and candy seemed very special. There were smiles in abundance when Santa showed up.

One downside was the fact that some children returned to their families for a visit during the holidays. Unfortunately, I was not one of them. The Sisters made an attempt to compensate by creating special meals for those kids who remained. It took away some of the hurt.

With the advantage of hindsight, I think that a group home was not such a bad place to be raised and, in many respects, was superior to foster care. We would get college-aged kids in as counselors each summer, and they were always fun to be around. It was not unusual to get to spend a weekend or two with friends or relatives of Sister Wilma, which was very nice. I remember driving out to Northumberland, Pa., with Sister Wilma to attend the wedding and reception of Orv Wright, who married one of the summer counselors.

Not all the decisions I made at Tabor were sound. Shortly after I entered high school, I agreed to be part of a plan that involved running away from the Home. Mary Covey and I were the "innocent" members of the conspiracy, while Kay Welch was the brains behind the caper. We departed late afternoon and were picked up by four local boys who had cars. As darkness descended and with no real plan as to our destination, Mary and I had a change of heart and requested transport home. Sister Wilma was anything but pleased and sarcastically commented, "Well, aren't you the good girls for returning home?" We both received the silent treatment for several days as a punishment. Kay changed her name and attempted to start a new life in Lansdale, but her plan backfired when she used her social security number to get a job. The authorities returned her after 30 days on the run.

About the same time frame, I had life-altering insight. It occurred at the bus stop while waiting for the high school bus. One of the trailer-park girls named Alice caustically commented to me, "You're just a Home kid, so who cares anyway." I smiled inwardly and realized I was much better off than Alice. That episode stayed with me a long time and gave me added confidence during my high school days.

The transition to high school was not difficult, because I had any number of friends and enjoyed the social side of school. I would have been better off if I had studied a little harder and received better than the average marks I brought home. Like many teenagers, I was self-absorbed and self-conscious about my looks and dress. I hated riding on the bus to church on Sunday, because of the Tabor Home emblazoned on the side. I was sure everyone was looking and smirking behind our backs. In hindsight I realize nobody cared one way or the other.

My mother died during my junior year in high school. Up until then, I had a fuzzy plan to live with her after graduating from school. For the first time, I started to worry that I didn't have a post-high school plan and that I was completely on my own as a rather unsophisticated 18-year-old. During that last year in school, I toned down quite a bit and became a little more introspective.

The last few years I lived at Tabor, I was fortunate enough to get some weekend baby-sitting jobs with the president of the Tabor Home Board of Directors, Dr. McKinney. Not only did this give me some spending money, but it also allowed me to hone my skills as a mother's helper and gave me an excellent work reference. Upon graduation, I obtained employment with Jim and Nancy Conley in Devon, Pa., as a live-in baby sitter and mother's helper. They could not have been more kind and understanding. Meanwhile, I enrolled at Wilford Academy studying cosmetology and successfully completed the course. Everything seemed to click, and I am convinced that God had a plan for me. The Conleys were perfect role models for me.

In 1969 I married a terrific guy named Tom McKelvey and had a little girl, Sarah Joy, three years later. We attend a wonderful church. God is good. While my life is not without problems, for the most part it is full and happy. Sometimes, dreams do come true!

Pattie Potter came to Tabor in 1946 at the age of 4. She left in 1960 after graduating from Central Bucks High School. She is married and the mother of one girl. She and her husband Tom reside in Berkley Heights, N.J.

SUNDAYS WERE THE WORST DAYS
By Mary Wilson Schaffer

My tale starts several years before I came to Tabor Home. All six sisters in the Wilson family were sent to foster homes in the Bucks County area. The three youngest (including me) were sent together in one home, but within a year my two older sisters were relocated to a home in Newtown while I was sent to the Skiff home in Upper Black Eddy. After 18 months, the social worker, Mrs. Stead, delivered me to Tabor. The year was 1950. I was 7 years old, in the second grade and scared to death. The memory of sitting with Miss Evelyn in the admin building, right after my arrival, is distinct and vivid. I was in tears and didn't have a clue as to what was going on. I thought the next step would be to lock me up in a room with bars on the windows. She did her best to quiet my fears and walked me to the girls' dorm and down the hallway to a four-bed room. I don't remember my roommates but the healing process must have begun, because things seemed much better after that.

I was a very happy kid at Tabor, and I never regretted going there. Otherwise, I wouldn't have had a home. I made a lot of friends my own age and admired the older girls like Bette Simon and Doris Gold. As I reflect, I can think of a lot of really good times I had in my childhood. They took us to the Ice Capades and the circus when it came to town. The police department used to put on Christmas dinners, and they would hand out gifts to all the children. It was wonderful!

The one inescapable fact that I faced every week was that I was on my own with no support from my family. While parents of other children came to Tabor on Sundays, the usual visiting days, I watched with envy at their seemingly idyllic relationship. Sundays were definitely the worst days.

My first foster parents, Paul and Elsie Beck, kept in touch with me with letters during the years I was in the Home. Their concern meant a lot to me, and I became quite attached to them. Paul died in 1955, but I remained close to Elsie for more than 50 years.

My sister Jean joined me at Tabor in 1954 but only stayed about two years. She was raised as a Roman Catholic, and religion seemed to get in the way at the Lutheran Tabor Home. Sister Wilma looked into transferring Jean to a home run by the Catholic Church and gave Jean the choice to leave, which she took. I was also offered the same opportunity, but by then I knew the system, had made a lot of friends and had no desire to start life anew.

The skills necessary to survive in a children's home are similar to those in a large, disciplined family. The happiest are those that don't break the rules, show concern for their family members and take a positive attitude about living. The unhappiest are those who resent authority, are selfish and self-centered and focus on the negative aspects of life. Fortunately, I was a straight arrow, never talked back to the Sisters or counselors and always wore a happy face.

I recall being very close to Sister Edith, the boys' housemother from the Virgin Islands, as well as Mrs. Krieger, one of the lay counselors. I also got along well with Edward Healy and his wife, supervisors in the boys' dorm.

Transition to high school did not come easy. I was at the age where I was agitated at my family situation, and studies were not important to me. The downside to that attitude was that it did not track with Sister Wilma's priority, and her values trumped mine. I was essentially grounded until my grades improved. It even got so bad that I had to bring notes home from my high school teachers stating my work was satisfactory.

Jimmy Jeffries was the only Home boy in my class in elementary and high school. We were on the safety patrol together, and we proudly wore those silver badges of authority. ("You don't cross the road until I tell you to cross the road. OK?") In 1961, at 17 years of age, I graduated from Central Bucks and was left with no forward plan regarding my life. Other than an occasional baby-sitting job for a lawyer in Chestnut Hill, I had no marketable skills for supporting myself.

Still living at the Home, I decided to sneak out after curfew and meet up with a Tabor boy that I was dating. Before the party got underway, I found out that someone had informed the authorities of the plot, so I scurried back to my bed just before Sister Wilma conducted a midnight bed check. Even though I won the battle of wits, I found out the following day I had lost the war. She informed me that she had contacted my sister in Levittown, Pa., and I was to pack my bags and depart immediately. Not the kind of "going away" party I would have chosen.

After two unhappy years with no job, no car and sponging off my sister, I made the move back to Doylestown and bunked with a high school friend, Ann Rounding, and her family. I obtained employment and went through several "character-building" experiences that seem to be a necessary part of the maturing process.

In 1975 I finally got it right and married Lawrence Schaffer, and we have created a happy life together. I wouldn't recommend my route for everyone, but it worked for me and "all's well that end's well."

Mary Wilson arrived at Tabor Home in 1950 at the age of 7 and graduated 10 years later. She is married to her husband Larry, and they live in Doylestown.

Chapter Five - The 1960s

IT WAS AMAZING HOW CLEAN TABOR WAS
By Commander Ed Bye, United States Navy

It didn't take long for a normal family of seven children, living in Newtown, Pa., to turn into a dysfunctional unit. Heavy drinking on the part of our father created an environment that caused our mother to depart and several siblings to become truants from school. An anonymous phone call to Child Welfare, relating our situation, resulted in three of us being sent to Tabor Home in September of 1968.

My initial reaction to Tabor was how amazingly clean it was. And I was stunned how much food there was to eat. I had no sooner checked in than I was on my way to Doylestown to get a haircut and some new clothes. All the kids made me feel quite welcome. My younger brother Michael and I shared a room on the second floor. All in all, it was a comfortable first day.

My strong work ethic had already been established by the time I arrived at the Home. Ever since I was 11 years old, I was bagging groceries and stocking shelves for a local supermarket. While residing at the Home, I was fortunate to hold jobs at Kenny's Newsstand, Servins' Catering and at the high school I attended. During the summer months I worked performing custodial tasks at Central Bucks West that resulted in a position with a lawn service company, owned by the husband of one of the teachers. It certainly helped to have spending money when there was neither parental financial assistance nor allowances provided at the time.

Most people who knew me in high school would characterize me as average. Realizing I wanted to make a difference, I ran for class president in junior high school. Having just arrived in the school district, I didn't really know many people and was close to very few. I graduated 212 out of 224 high school classmates. As I reflect, that might indicate a little below average. I have always enjoyed reading, and that has been a big advantage over the years.

Perhaps I was responding to my own low expectations, but I never even thought about attending college. I took no college preparatory classes. Instead I participated in the DECCA Program, which was a work-study program designed for students who were not on the traditional college track. In my senior year I attended classes in the morning and technical classes in the afternoon. Three days a week I worked at Sears and Roebuck in Doylestown in lieu of attending classes. My rather hazy goal was to become a social worker, inspired by my respect for Emma Smith, my social worker. I did not realize that, at a minimum, a bachelor's degree was required.

I don't want to give the impression that I was exempt from work at Tabor, just because I had jobs outside the walls. Quite the contrary, one finished the inside work first before taking on the extracurricular paying tasks.

To the best of my recollection, there were approximately 30 boys and 30 girls living at Tabor during my five-year stint. We all established a fairly tight, family-like relationship, treating each other like brothers and sisters.

The whole tone of Tabor changed in the last few years I was there. Sister Wilma retired and was replaced by Sister Gunnell Sterner. My memory is a bit hazy, but shortly thereafter Sister Gunnell was replaced by a social worker, and the concept of firm discipline was discarded. There were still some very competent counselors on staff who were positive role models; Ms. Guest and Donald McGregor and his wife Bonnie come to mind.

Sundays at Tabor were the worst. That was visiting day for parents, and it really brought home to the Bye clan the realization that our father was often banned from the grounds as a result of his failed sobriety. My mother never visited in the five years I was at the Home. For a 15- or 16-year old, this was stark reality at a very basic level.

In 1973, shortly after graduating from Central Bucks, I joined the U.S. Navy as a Hospital Corpsman and advanced through the enlisted ranks to Chief Petty Officer. While enlisted, I obtained my college degree (and eventually two master's degrees), and was commissioned a naval officer in July 1985. By the time I retired in February 2005, I had completed 32 years of naval service.

I have two wonderful and successful daughters plus a lovely granddaughter. I am quite pleased the way my life has played out. I often think of my upbringing at Tabor Home and realize that many people that I know had it a whole lot worse.

My overall impression of the five years I spent at Tabor Home remains a positive one. I have met and worked with many individuals who did not have as fortunate an upbringing as my family members and me. I am certain I would have not have been as successful in life had it not been for the years I spent at Tabor Home.

Ed Bye came to Tabor in 1968 with his older sister Sandy and his younger brother Michael at the age of 14. He left after graduating from high school five years later. He is a retired Commander in the U.S. Navy, has two grown daughters and lives in Stafford, Va.

MY NICKNAME WAS DEVIL'S DISCIPLE
By Fred Auditor

I don't remember life before Tabor Home and have no recollection of my mother or father. I know I was an only child, and in 1954, at 4 years of age, a social worker brought me to Tabor as a ward of the Commonwealth of Pennsylvania. One of my earliest memories was sitting on the big window ledge on the second floor of the boys' dorm and watching parents visit or pick up their children on Sunday afternoon. I would daydream that one of my parents would show up and we would have this marvelous reunion. Of course, no visitor ever materialized, and my childish fantasy transformed into the grim reality that orphans never get visits from parents on Sunday.

A situation that occurred several years later would have altered my life in a dramatic fashion except for a "Catch 22" law on the state books. After observing me working during a Tabor Home May Day celebration, a local millionaire (I was told he invented and patented the game of Monopoly) told the head administrator he wanted to adopt me. The deal fell through when no relative could be contacted to sign the release papers. I occasionally reminisce what life would have been like as the son in a really wealthy family.

Tabor Home was full of traditions. Some were worthwhile and uplifting, such as prayers before meals and bedtime, mandatory baseball games after evening meal in the summer, and celebrating Christmas with presents, bountiful feasts and joyous hymns. Other traditions were less admirable. The initiation of all "new kids" was one. Mine consisted of being taken up to the woods at sunset and being persuaded to climb a ladder to the top of the Tabor reservoir. The reservoir was a concrete cylinder about 20 feet in diameter, located about eight feet above ground level and perched on top a huge mound of dirt sloping up to the base of the structure. When I reached the top of the water tank, the ladder was removed, and I was left high and dry and scared to death. After reviewing my alternatives (sleeping on top all night, jumping to my death, crying, or hanging over the side and just breaking my leg) I opted for the latter, let go my grip and hoped for the best. I survived the fall, but I had no idea how to get out of the woods and back to my bed. By this time it was quite dark, so I stumbled in the direction of the most light. My strategy worked and my initiation was over.

I was accepted into the fraternity of Tabor kids. I couldn't wait to grow up and continue the tradition of new kid initiation.

My first impression of Tabor was how big the place was and the fact that there were so many children there. Everything was super size from eating meals in one huge dining hall to sleeping in an open dormitory with more than 20 other kids ranging in age from 4 or 5 up to about 12 or 13. After that age, they moved you to the back room, which consisted of about 10 additional beds. The "barn boys" would reside in the back room, so the aroma of the cows was often present.

Sister Wilma Loehrig was the head deaconess at Tabor, and she took an instant liking to me from the day I enrolled. She and others referred to me as the Littlest Angel, which was the name of a children's play that was occasionally performed by the Home kids. As I grew up and got into some un-angel-like mischief, my nickname changed to the Devil's Disciple.

Corporal punishment was quite common at Tabor, especially in the boys' house. Spare the rod and spoil the child was an unspoken rule among staff members. One heavy-set woman counselor was quite adept at utilizing drumsticks to prevent children in her charge from becoming spoiled. During one such episode, I snatched the stick from her hand and responded in kind. Another full-time staff member was particularly physical. This former Chief Petty Officer in the U.S. Navy treated us as if we were in boot camp. His technique for finding guilty parties was to punish the entire group until someone came forward. After peer pressure procured a confession, the perpetrator would pass between two rows of appointed disciplinarians. Their punching, kicking and slapping were strong incentives to behave righteously. (This individual was asked to leave when there was a change in administration a year after I graduated.)

I do not want to imply that all of the punishment we received was unwarranted. I remember several of the barn boys stealing bicycles in Doylestown, repainting them and hiding them in the haymow in the barn. Tabor kids were banned from owning bikes after a car on Route 611, right in front of the gate, hit a bike rider. The local police were aware of the ban and pulled several of us over during a bike ride on New Britain Road. They recovered the bikes and returned them to their rightful owners. No charges were filed. I was always surprised how lenient the cops were whenever any Tabor kids were caught violating the law. Maybe it was more productive just to turn the problem over to Sister Wilma, who was quite effective in controlling her kids.

Ensuring that all the children received a good education was one of the Home's primary goals. Study hall was mandatory for everyone, and an adult supervisor was always available for homework assistance. Nevertheless, from a kid's perspective, school was not a very friendly place. Both the teachers and other children tended to look down on Tabor kids. One had to excel in something in order to be accepted. It was also very hard to convince anyone to be your girlfriend when you had zero money to spend. I chose to try to standout in sports. It worked reasonably well. I lettered in football, playing safety on the varsity team that went undefeated my senior year. I also ran the quarter mile, the mile and the mile relay. The team was good enough to be invited to compete in the Franklin Relays in Philadelphia. I was quite proud of my reputation as a Central Bucks athlete.

My post-Tabor days are interesting. After graduating in 1968 from Central Bucks High School, I was lifeguarding at Ocean City, N.J., when I received my draft notice. They bussed me to Philadelphia for induction. I couldn't verify that I was the last surviving member of my family (which would have given me a deferment), and I was not interested in taking a free bus to Canada to avoid the Southeast Asia conflict, so I enlisted in the Army for two years.

Shortly after arriving in Vietnam, I was in a firefight and had my leg shot up. After a hospital rehabilitation period, I was given a disability discharge. I got married, had two boys (Joseph and Daniel) and started working at a steel mill. That marriage failed, but my next one was a success. This union produced a son and twin daughters.

As I look back at my years at Tabor I have mixed feelings, but the overriding memory is positive. Tabor Home did a lot for me. It gave me a place to live, a good value system and took care of me when I needed it. I have never smoked and don't consume alcohol. I benefited from my association with all the other kids I met there and received a great education.

On the downside, Tabor was a physical environment and a lot of hitting took place. It left no physical scars, but some were undoubtedly left with mental ones. Instead of trying to understand why young children wet the bed, the staff used humiliation by having the child wash the soiled sheets and hanging them on the clothesline for all the other kids to see. It was not uncommon to discipline a child by putting him in a closet for hours. I also had a traumatic incident in which the local minister could not keep his hands to himself when I was functioning as an altar boy. To a young boy with no family support network, this was just another hurdle I had to overcome. I reported the encounter, but to no avail.

One positive outcome was it convinced me that hitting children was not productive, and I am proud of never resorting to violence in raising my own children. I had no paternal role model while growing up, so I had to play that role by ear.

On many occasions I have told my children that I wished they could spend some time at Tabor Home for both the experience and the knowledge that living in a normal family is as good as it gets.

Fred Auditor came to Tabor at age 4 and remained through his graduation from Central Bucks High in 1968. The father of five children and two stepchildren, Fred now lives in Scottsdale, Ariz., with his wife Judy. He is presently in rehabilitation for an injury sustained while driving a city bus.

THE UPS AND DOWNS OF LIFE AT TABOR
By Donna Dumm McDonald

I was one of those "lifers" who came to Tabor at age 3 and stayed until completing high school. My entire childhood was spent there, and I can't even remember life prior to 1956. I was not alone, because my 5-year-old brother Eddie and big sister Sharon (age 7) accompanied me. My first few nights were spent in tears, until fatigue overtook me and I finally got to sleep. Part of my fear was being separated from my sister whom I looked upon as a personal bodyguard and problem-solver. She was assigned a room with other girls her age, and I slept with the pre-schoolers. Even if Sharon couldn't have acted as a surrogate mother, she would have brought me great comfort had we roomed together.

My mother had been working in Doylestown and trying to support three kids by herself. With the wages paid to women in those days, it was only a matter of time before she had to give us up, because she did not have the wherewithal to keep the family together.

As in any child's life, there were up days as well as down days at Tabor. The memories of Christmas and May Day are quite distinct. I remember how wonderful I felt walking into the dining room the night Tabor celebrated Christmas and looking at the stage filled with wrapped gifts of all shapes and sizes. The Willow Grove Naval Base would host a separate party and hand out presents. Christmas holidays seemed so magical with these events and many others.

May Day transformed Tabor from an institution to a giant fairground with booths selling handicrafts and other knickknacks, alumni greeting old friends, religious services on the lawn and dinner served to the public in the dining room. I remember dancing around the Maypole and thinking, "What a fabulous adventure."

Other positive memories were the kids involved with crafts in the summer, attending the New York World's Fair, playing baseball in the summer and husking corn on cold autumn Saturdays. Did I mention the thrill of kissing the boys on the back steps? Oh yes, and the counselor whose last job was with a Russian circus. She taught us all acrobatic tricks.

Some of the negative thoughts about Tabor were that some of the counselors were verbally or physically abusive to the children.

One counselor stands out as particularly inept. I remember her giving one of the girls, Debbie, a beating on a regular basis for no discernable reason. I thought Sister Wilma did a marvelous job as the director of the Home including getting rid of counselors that conducted themselves in inappropriate ways. I realize how difficult her job was in being responsible for the welfare and security of 80 children.

We had our share of just plain miserable juveniles that were one step from reform school before they showed up at Tabor (even if it wasn't necessarily their fault). They made all our lives pretty unbearable. Most of them didn't last too long at the Home. There were also a number of just unhappy kids that ran away if they got the chance, even though this didn't happen often. It seemed as if someone was missing from bed check every once in a while. When they returned (which they almost always did), they were never punished. It was almost as if the event never took place. One particular boy, who used his bike as his get-away vehicle, fell into the quarry and killed himself.*

As I was the youngest child at Tabor at that time, Sister Wilma seemed to adopt me and treat me as her pet. Of course I was very pleased being her favorite. I also remember when some of the alumni would return to the Home and show real concern. Joe and Bobby Hoppe were two who kept in touch with me, even though they had left Tabor years before. It was very nice to have "big brothers" caring about you.

Although I was the designated "pet" while growing up, the honor did not extend into high school. I developed a love-hate relationship with Sister Wilma (as most teenagers do with the parent figure) that culminated in her not attending my graduation ceremony. She objected to my choice in boyfriends, which I could not accept. (I married the guy and got divorced two years later. Maybe she was a better judge of character than I was.)

The bottom line is that Tabor shaped my character and value system. I am quite pleased with the way I turned out. I get along well with all classes of people, and I have a strong sense of community service. I also feel blessed that I had a home while growing up, and I received better care there than a lot of children did in their own family. My sister Sharon does not share my opinion. She was quite sad that our mother put her in the Home, but that's another story.

I truly believe that I am what God wanted me to be. I will admit to struggling in the development of parenting skills in a home setting for lack of a parenting husband/wife role model. But, all in all, I am quite pleased with my upbringing and adult life. Thank you, Tabor Home and all those who contributed to my development.

* This incident could not be verified.

Donna Dumm came to Tabor as a 3-year-old in 1956 and left in 1969. She is the mother of one son who is pursuing his master's degree at the University of Maryland. She lives in Pottstown, Pa., with her husband James.

VIEW FROM THE TOP
By Sister Gunnel Sterner

When I received a call in 1969 to relieve Sister Wilma Loehrig as the head matron at Tabor Home, I accepted it willingly but with some reservations. I was aware that Sister Wilma had served as the Chief Executive Officer at Tabor for so many years that her name was inextricably linked with the Home. Yet I also realized that the position couldn't help but burn out the incumbent and, in this case, she was more than ready for retirement. The responsibilities associated with running an institution of up to 80 children from broken homes were tremendous. However, I would not be truthful if I did not confess to looking forward to the challenge. The opportunity to affect so many children's lives in a positive manner occurs only once in a lifetime of service.

I was serving in Philadelphia at the Lutheran Children and Family Services organization, so I was well schooled in the problems of child welfare. I had visited Tabor on several occasions such as sauerkraut suppers and May Day festivities, so I was familiar with the grounds and physical plant. I knew Sister Wilma fairly well, so the turnover was quite painless. I was in a hurry to get on with it, and she had no desire to remain and see if I knew what I was doing. Thus, in short order, I was the third deaconess in charge of Tabor Home in the past 55 years. Before us was Sister Lena Beideck, who served from 1914 until 1942.

The children I was totally responsible for were, for the most part, normal. That is, they had all come from broken homes and were damaged to some extent when they arrived. They went to school, played sports, carried out assigned chores, went to Sunday school and church, were not in trouble with the law, spoke their mind, liked to argue and negotiate. The girls were more difficult to deal with than the boys. It was obvious to me that Sister Wilma preferred dealing with the male population and did not pretend to hide her bias.

It did not take long for reality to set in. The physical plant needed maintenance and repair. Some of the staff were not qualified to handle troubled youths. In my opinion, the board of directors did not appear to have the welfare of the children as their prime objective. There never seemed to be enough money for the care and feeding of the children, upgrading the facilities, maintaining the grounds and the farm, and paying livable salaries for the staff. In addition, changes in society were occurring regarding child welfare. There was almost consensus among professional psychologists that foster care was far superior (and cheaper) than institutionalizing needy children. Just as if I were a substitute teacher in high school, the children tested me right away. Within the first two weeks, several of the girls ran away. The next day I got a phone call from one of them. She asked for transportation home. My answer was short and direct. You managed to get where you are without my help; you can return without my help; and if you want to remain living here, I had better see you within 24 hours. Lo and behold, they all showed up by the deadline. The comment from the boys was, "That was really stupid."

With the advantage of 20-20 hindsight, I realize the die was already cast when I showed up at Tabor Home. Others realized sooner than I, that I would be the last designated head deaconess at Tabor. Only my tenure was unknown. It did not help my longevity that I was outspoken about the needs of the Home or that I was critical of the board. Within two years I was asked to give up my post. It was one of the most disappointing days of my life.

I could divide the challenges in two categories. The first was how to make life more tolerable for the children. One of my first acts after taking the reins was to ask several of the staff to leave. They were simply not qualified to handle problem youth. A boot-camp mentality may work for the military, but in a children's home it created quite a hostile environment and I considered it counterproductive. The next thing I did was to become an advocate for the kids at school. I certainly got the impression the teachers took advantage of them, because they had no parent to represent them. In those two years I attended 42 teachers conferences acting on their behalf. Also in high school the established policy was that no Tabor kids were permitted to take drivers' education. After my objection to such a prejudicial policy, the administrators changed the rules. Another time a group of our high school kids wanted to participate in the March of Dimes to fight polio, but they could not get any sponsors to assist. I had some of the children bring the problem to the board of directors, and they voted to spend $175 for the children's march. Forty-two very proud marchers participated. That aspect of my job was quite satisfying. I could make a difference in the lives of a lot of children.

The second category was maintaining the facilities. Two weeks after I reported for duty, the boiler in the girls' house blew up. Twenty-two girls were without heat or hot water. This was a dramatic crisis, which had to be addressed immediately. Upgrading and fixing the physical plant was a constant and long-term worry. When I accepted the job, I did not envision that so much of my time would be spent begging for money.

The president of the board was Dr. McKinney in 1969, and he was a strong supporter of having a Lutheran deaconess in charge. Sadly, he died a year later, and the remaining board members did not share his opinion.

One of the downsides of my position was the loneliness of command. Not only was there no one with which to share the burdens of being a "mother" to an army of needy children, but also receiving a thank you or a pat on the back from anyone was unheard of. I can't tell you how welcome a supportive phone call or a note of appreciation would have been after a 100-hour week of solving problems and negotiating among warring groups. The closest I came was a phone call I received from a former child after I had left Tabor. The person identified herself as a mother now, and she said she wanted to let me know that she realized that I was right about a lot of things.

My concluding thoughts are that my two years at the Home were filled with many memories, both positive and negative. I know I influenced a lot of children and made their lives happier. I am quite proud of all the kids that moved on and led successful lives. I doubt that transferring authority from a religious-based institution to a secular one was beneficial. Several years after my departure, I asked one of the remaining children how things had changed. She replied, "We don't have to go to church anymore." To which I say, "How sad!"

Sister Gunnel Sterner was the head matron at Tabor Home from 1969 until 1971. She is presently retired and living in Bethlehem, Pa.

Chapter Six - The 1970s & 1980s

I WISH I HAD STAYED UNTIL I WAS 18
By Robert Somershoe

We Somershoe brothers came to Tabor in 1971, because our parents weren't very skilled in parenting. There were three of us. William was 10 years old, Brian was 6 and I was 7 when the social worker picked us up from a temporary foster home in Bucks County and deposited us at Tabor Home. I remember being terrified at this markedly different environment. I quickly learned the "pecking order" system and adjusted to it. Also it was reassuring to know that I could count on being fed each and every day. It probably took a month or two to completely adjust to my new stable life style.

Even though I was only a year older, I felt responsibility to look after Brian. There were a number of boys around our age and we hung out more with them than with William, who found friends his own age.

Attendance at school seemed to be optional with my real family. The foster home parents didn't seem to care whether we went every day either. So attending elementary school full-time came as a surprise, but I recall that school was a positive experience in my life.

I was impressed with the Lutheran sisters like Sister Edna, who supervised the children the first few years I lived at the Home. I did not like the head administrator. She was the chief disciplinarian, and most kids did their best to avoid her. She lived over the laundry room with her little dachshund Oscar. Of course, we all came in contact with her at meal times.

The transition of Tabor from a religious-based home to a secular one was interesting, but I didn't have a great awareness at the time it was happening. The discipline definitely trended downward, and the social workers used a carrot approach (demerit system) instead of a stick to control behavior. As long as you kept your nose clean, you were given privileges. To be fair, the clientele changed pretty dramatically after the Sisters left. Inner-city children, exposed to a more violent childhood environment, were transported to the Home from Philadelphia. In short order, the simple life in rural Bucks County was transformed. The new rules permitted anyone over 14 years old to smoke cigarettes, and some of the older kids used drugs. In my opinion, Tabor was getting a bad reputation, and all the kids were definitely looked down upon. We were divided up after sixth grade and sent to various junior high schools in an attempt to minimize groups of Tabor kids at one school.

Even though there were occasional fights among ourselves, we had exceptional *esprit de corps*. We would defend aggressively any Tabor kid who faced any kind of outside conflict.

In 1979, after eight years at Tabor, Brian and I left the Home to live with my mother, who had established a more stable living condition. Looking back, I realize the move was a mistake. The living condition turned unstable, and I was emancipated at age 16. I wish I had stayed at Tabor until I was 18 and had been able to graduate from Central Bucks High School.

After dropping out, I joined the Air Force and subsequently earned my General Equivalency Diploma.

Robert Somershoe arrived at Tabor Home with his two brothers in 1971 at age 7. He left eight years later. He presently lives in Philadelphia with his wife Suzette and five children.

TABOR WAS A GREAT PLACE TO LIVE
By Brian Somershoe

My brothers and I spent our early years in various foster homes. For the most part, the families were mean. However, the very last family was quite nice. I was in a bedroom with two other boys, and they had a son my age that I got along with quite well. So I was not thrilled when I had to gather up all my belongings in Bensalem, Pa., where I was living, to be shipped off to Tabor Home. The year was 1971, and I was 6 years old. My two older brothers, William (10) and Robert (7), made the trip with me.

My first impression of Tabor was there was a distinct lack of privacy. The showers did not have doors, and we had community bathrooms. Modesty played no part in a Tabor boy's life. The first few weeks were confusing, but I had been bounced around in life so I was able to adjust fairly quickly. It helped that Robert was around for assistance. I did not know what a normal family life consisted of, but I recall missing my grandmother. For a number of years I was the youngest boy at Tabor. I just stayed flexible and went with the flow. It proved to be a good strategy.

Life under the supervision of Lutheran nuns was certainly bearable. By and large they were caring and nice to the children. One exception was the head administrator. She was there just a short while, but she had a reputation for using a belt for punishment. I had first-hand knowledge of her disciplinarian approach when I dropped food on the floor while sitting at her table. I can't remember whether I just picked it up or popped it into my mouth, but whatever it was, it upset her greatly. I do remember paying the price for my error.

Another time I accidentally broke a storm window that was ready for installation. I either stepped on it or threw an errant ball through the pane. The belt was used in retribution for the broken window.

As soon as social workers took charge of the Home, they instituted a point system for control. There were five category levels, and each child was graded on a weekly basis. Level one (the most prestigious level) was awarded for those children who accumulated fewer than five demerits per week. The categories were cooperation, language and attitude. Level five was awarded for those getting more than 20 demerits. Skipping school or getting caught shoplifting were common reasons for changing levels. A single incident with a counselor involving intemperate language could accumulate demerits in all categories rapidly. I seem to recall that my brother Robert was often in the bottom category. I was almost always at level one and was given $5 gift certificates to King's department store or invited to play miniature golf in town or allowed to go horseback riding or even go skiing. It was a good life if you behaved yourself and established a reputation as a level one performer. Tabor was a great place to live!

School always was easy for me, and I consistently had A's and B's in both elementary and junior high school. I was put into the gifted program at Kutz Elementary and did quite well. I, along with most Tabor kids, felt it was demeaning when free lunches were publicly handed out at school, and classmates snickered at the "less fortunate" receiving welfare.

Even though I enjoyed living at Tabor, there were several things that could have been better. I was entrapped in a "Catch 22" situation when we were split up to various junior high schools. Because I went to Lenape, I had to catch the high school bus, which prevented me from attending my first period Latin class. I was given a failing grade, despite my protestations about the unfairness of the situation. I had no advocate to fight this obvious injustice.

Whether it was academics or athletics, low expectations for Tabor kids and the lack of a support group created an environment that did not encourage high performance. While wrestling for the Warrington Athletic Association in the 105-pound weight class, I received a number of medals and even fought an opponent (who later went to Penn State) to a tie. Yet there was no one around to encourage me to bigger and better things.

I left the Home when my mother felt she could supervise two teen-age boys at her home. The decision to take Robert and me from Tabor was ill-advised and did not work out. I ended up fending for myself in a big city high school for my junior and senior year. I was certainly bright enough to go to college, but there was no one available to give me direction or encouragement. In retrospect, I regret never getting my bachelor's degree or even attempting the challenge of higher education.

Brian Somershoe came to Tabor Home in 1971 as a 6-year-old with his two older brothers, William and Robert. He left eight years later. He presently lives in Bensalem with his wife April and their two children.

TABOR WAS THE TURNING POINT IN MY LIFE
By Charles Waller

As an 11-year-old living with my parents in Florida, I thought my family was fairly normal. We visited Disney World that year and I was instructed by my mother to meet her at the car at a specific time. When I failed to show at the appointed hour, she drove home without me. After an hour or so I turned myself in to security, and they contacted social services. I was put in a shelter for runaway children while the authorities contacted my mother. After a two-week negotiation period, I was put on a bus for the trip back home. My mother's maternal instincts were evidently not well developed.

The following year my parents separated for perhaps the twentieth time. My brother and I left Florida for Bensalem, Pa., with my father. He was a paraplegic and needed constant medical assistance from V.A. hospitals. With neither parent in a position to care for me, I was sent to Trenton, N.J., to live with an aunt. Neither she nor I were very happy with the relationship, so the following year I hitchhiked across the Delaware River and turned myself over to a social worker in Bensalem. (One lesson I had learned in Florida was that the state government must look after you if your parents are unable or unwilling.) She petitioned the court to allow me to become a ward of the Commonwealth of Pennsylvania, and I was placed at Tabor in the summer of 1980.

Although I was unaware of the situation at the time, Tabor was transitioning from a "live-in" institution to one that worked with locating foster families for needy children. I was one of only eight or nine boys and a like number of females living there full-time.

My first day was memorable. My mental state was positive. I was glad to be there. My feeling was that Tabor was the key to a good education, which was my primary goal at the time. The staff ensured I was fed, and then they bought me a wardrobe. I had arrived with just the clothes on my back, nothing else. The kids made me feel welcome, and I sensed we had an unspoken kinship, as we were all in the same boat.

Meals were taken in the cafeteria located in the girls' dorm. Food was served family-style, and all 16 children participated, along with the staff. I had a sense of contentment and belonging. Free time was spent in leisure activities such as playing basketball, arts and crafts, running and swimming. On occasion, some staff members would take us fishing. Our chores consisted of making our bed and keeping our rooms straightened up. There were no farming duties, and I don't think Tabor was even operating a farm by that time.

When school started in September, I was placed in a foster family. They were quite religious, and I was placed in a private church school. Before the year was over, I requested and was granted permission to return to Tabor. Most of the kids I lived with in 1980 were still there the next summer.

I was then placed into the home of Wynona Vrancken, a single white mother living in Chalfont, Pa. I am African-American, and there were some cultural differences, in addition to adolescent - parent conflicts. When I needed a change from living with her, Wynona was careful that I not feel abandoned. She asked her sister-in-law Diane West to share her Doylestown home with me until I was ready to return to Wynona. Also I was in periodic contact with a Tabor social worker (Jodi Donovan) who ensured that both the courts and I were satisfied with the living conditions.

As I look back, I realize that Wynona was always there for me. It's so important for an adolescent to have an adult to lean on, and I found I could always talk to her. Also as I began to excel in athletics at high school, she encouraged me. Our relationship improved with time, and I remain close to her to this day. The middle name of my daughter is Wynona.

I graduated from Central Bucks West High School in the class of 1985 after several successful basketball seasons. I was the starting center my senior year, even though I was only 6 feet 1 inch tall. Our team won the league championship my junior year, the only basketball championship in school history.

Later I earned a bachelor's degree at Temple University, majoring in psychology. Knowing how important it is for teenagers to have caring adults in their lives, I spent my early career working with adolescents in the juvenile justice system, advocating, counseling and providing outward bound and physical fitness programs.

While I did not spend a lot of time at Tabor, I am convinced that living there was the turning point for me. Prior to that, I was

171

hanging out with a crowd that was constantly in trouble with the law. I was impressed how well the staff at Tabor looked after me. I am forever thankful for their efforts and concern.

Charles Waller came to live at Tabor in 1980 at the age of 13. He was placed in several foster homes but maintained contact with Tabor until high school graduation. He married his wife Olabisi in Africa. They have an 2-year-old son, Charles Jr., and infant daughter, and live in New Britain, Pa. For the past three years he was the owner/operator of Neo Dekor Contemporary Furniture in Philadelphia. Recently, he has pursued international business opportunities.

AFTERWORD

As Tabor Children's Services celebrates its 100th anniversary, the agency, in 2007, is serving the needs of many consumers, but in a different way from the past as described in this book. While Tabor Home was a residential facility, the Tabor of today provides community-based services from its two locations. The Doylestown site, still located on Route 611, houses administrative offices, a child care center with 100 children and social work offices for Bucks County programs. The child care center provides the option of affordable daycare that was not available to families whose children grew up at Tabor Home. Tabor social workers serve Bucks County children and families in their homes, and this in-home program has a high success rate for keeping families intact while maintaining child safety. Life skills specialists provide training for Bucks County adolescents who are preparing to leave the child welfare system and help prevent youth homelessness. In fact, Orv Wright has brought his professional insights to job interview and resume seminars in this life skills program, and conveys to today's youth that, like him, they can leave the system and succeed in life. Many direct services are also delivered from Tabor's Philadelphia office located in the city's Germantown section. These services include foster care, special needs adoption, in-home services, outpatient mental health and independent living for adolescents. The agency also delivers school-based services in North Philadelphia and provides a small group facility for autistic adult males. Tabor operates with a $12,000,000 budget, a staff of 150 and a dedicated board of trustees, and is one of the largest providers of child welfare services in southeastern Pennsylvania.

William A. Haussmann, ACSW
Executive Director 1973 -

LIST OF ILLUSTRATIONS

#4 Children and deaconesses, including Sister Lena (far right, second row), ca. 1919

#5 Children and deaconesses, including Sister Lena (far left, second row), ca. 1927

#6 A young Frank Bell at Tabor Home, late 1920s

#7 Alumnus Frank Bell (seated center), reminiscing on the Tabor campus in 1992 with Kathryn Stafford, Harry Clark (standing) and Executive Director, William A. Haussmann

#8 Summer counselor George Breitling (at right) with resident, Otto Plequette (center), and another counselor at Tabor Home in the late 1930s

#9 Setting for Christmas in the administration building, ca. 1940

#10 Christmas Eve 1951, at Tabor Home (Clockwise, from lower left: Bobby Hoppe, Walter Evans, Orville Wright, Arnold Wenzloff, Ted Knauss, Wilbur Wright, Danny Burmeister, Don Fritz, a resident and Carl Hoppe)

#11 Don Fritz as a resident in 1953

#12 Don Fritz as an alumnus in 2002

#13 Alumnus Fred (Fritz) Strowig, the first president of the Tabor Alumni Association, which began in 1958

#14 Returning alumni at a May Day coffee booth at Tabor Home, 1963

#15 Residents at a May Day beverage booth at Tabor Home, 1963

#16 Executive Director William A. Haussmann, shortly after he came to Tabor in 1973

#17 Children playing basketball the late 1970s

#18 Children receiving home schooling at Tabor in the late 1970s

#19 Children around the pool on the Tabor campus during the 1980s

#20 Tabor Alumni at their August 1990 picnic at the home of Sarah Stafford Walker (Standing: Donald South, Thomas d'Arcy, Helen Berger Freas, Myrtle Berger Frazier, Charles Frankenfield, Don Fritz. Middle row: Otto Kinshofer, John Frankenfield, George Stafford, Kathy Berger Coulton, Ida Stafford Fenstermacher. Front row: Sarah Stafford Walker, Daisy Beck)

#21 Alumnus Bobby Hoppe and his wife Dottie, who visited the Tabor campus in 1995

#22 Walter (Lefty) Seibold and Harry Clark at the 2003 Tabor Alumni luncheon at the William Penn Inn

#23 Tabor Alumni at their October 2004 banquet on the Tabor campus (Standing, rear row: Robert Somershoe, Norman Raike, Harry Clark, Ted Fritz/family member, Ann Osgood Whiteside, Don Fritz, Orville Wright, Walter Evans. Standing, middle row: Rudolph Krause, Margaret Schmaltz Yost, Kathy Berger Coulton, Fred Strowig, Kay Welch Watson, Joan Bach Youells, an alumna, Catherine Kniese Choromanski, Joe Hoppe, James Kniese. Seated: Ernestine Strowig Pilant, Charles Frankenfield, Genevieve Friel Barrett, Peggy Welch, Pattie Potter McKelvey, Dorothy Maloney Buckner, Mary Wilson Schaffer. Kneeling: Daisy Beck)

#24 Layout of Tabor Home property, 1950s, in a 2005 drawing by alumnus John Freas

INDEX

Page numbers in **boldface** indicate the primary remembrance by or about the person indexed.

189

F

Fenstermacher, Ida Stafford, **8**, 9, 111; illus. #20

Fetzer, Jacob, 42

Frankenfield, Charles, **32-33**; illus. #20, #23

Frankenfield, Clara, 33

Frankenfield, John, 33, 110; illus. #20

Frankenfield, Mary, 33

Frazier, Myrtle Berger, 15, 16; illus. #20

Freas, John, **126-128**; illus. #24

Freas, Helen Berger, 15, 16; illus. #20

Freas, Walt, 126

Fretz, Philip A., iii, 4, 25, 82

Friel, Charles, 22, 23

Friel, Genevieve. *See* Barrett, Genevieve Friel

Fritz, Billie Jane. *See* Tindall, Jane Fritz

Fritz, Don, 75, 77, 78, 80, 86, 88, **104-106**, 107, 109-112; illus. #10, #11, #12, #20, #23

   visits Joe Hoppe, 75-81

Fritz, Martha Moyer, 75, **109-112**

G

Garonski, Mrs. (laundress), 60

George, Allen, 49

"God's Country" poem (d'Arcy), 28

Gold, Doris, 135, 139, 147

Gold, Rudy, 126, 127

Good, Albert, 55

Good, Jimmy, 61

Greenholt, Tracy, 109

Groman, Bill, 49

Guest, Ms. (counselor), 153

H

Harris, Polly Duckworth, 57, 58, 63, 68, 69, **70-72**

Haskey, Ben, 110

Haussmann, William, illus. #7, #16

Healy, Edward, 148

Highton, Jake, **40-51**, 52, 80, 85, 86, 89, 91, 92, 108

Hirschbuhl, Carol, 129, 131

Hirschbuhl, Ginny. *See* Carson, Ginny Hirschbuhl

Holidays and special days

Atlantic City trips, 66-67, 70, 80

birthdays, 8, 9, 25, 65, 67

Christmas, 7, 8, 28, 48, 65, 81, 91, 93, 97, 105-106, 110, 123, 124, 141, 144, 155, 159; illus. #9, #10

Easter, 6-7, 48, 67, 97, 122

Halloween, 6, 8, 16

May Day, 6, 8, 25-26, 31, 65-66, 97, 106, 110-111, 155, 159; illus. #14, #15

Hoppe, Bobby, 75, 86, 115, 160; illus. #10, #21

Hoppe, Carl, 49, 75, 77, 86, 105, 115, 125; illus. #10

writes to Sister Wilma, 123-124

Hoppe, Joe, 52, **75-81**, 86, 88, 115, 160; illus. #23

Hoppe, Sam, 79, 81

J

James, Virginia, 93

Jeffries, Jim, 126, 127, 148

K

Kinshofer, Otto, illus. #20

Kiwanis Club, 48

Knauss, Eddie, 77, 99, 102, 103, 115

Knauss, Marie, 97, 103, 107

Knauss, Richie, **102-103**, 115

Knauss, Ted, 103; illus. #10

Kniese, Catherine. *See* Choromanski, Catherine Kniese

Kniese, Bob, 97, 98, 113, 115

Kniese, Charles, 97, 98, 115

Kniese, James (Butch), 97, 98, **113-115**; illus. #23

Kohler, Jane, 49

Krause, Alvina, 20, 21

Krause, Kathleen, 21

Krause, Richard, 21

Krause, Rudolph, **20-21**; illus. #23

Krause, Walter, 20, 21

Krieger, Mrs. (counselor), 148

Kummer, Wilma, 65

Kutz, Martha, 64

Kutz, Paul, 35, 64

L

Lamartine, Reverend Philip, iii

Lawrey, Marylee, 136

Leatherman, Dick, 49

Loehrig, Sister Wilma, **118-125**; illus. #3

Bill Beck and, 29, 30

Catherine Kniese Choromanski and, 97, 98

Cathy Welch Watson and, 133, 134

Daisy Beck and, 31

discipline and, 80, 114

dogs of, 78, 126, 130

Don Fritz and, 77, 78, 109

Donna Dumm McDonald and, 160

Doris Gold and, 139

Dorothea Maloney Buckner and, 53, 79, 86

Emily Mumaw Brunk and, 73

Fred Auditor and, 156, 157

Ginny Hirschbuhl Carson and, 129, 130

Jake Highton and, 42

Jane Fritz Tindall and, 107-108

Joan Bach Youells and, 139

Joe Hoppe and, 77, 78

John Freas and, 127

Mary Wilson Schaffer and, 147-148

Orville Wright and, 77, 144

Pattie Potter McKelvey and, 144

Polly Duckworth Harris and, 71

Richie Knauss and, 102-103

Rudolph Krause and, 21

Sara Duckworth Carlson and, 61, 65, 66, 67, 68, 69

Sister's Emma's death and, 139

tenure at Tabor Home, 64, 84, 125

Tom d'Arcy and, 28

Somershoe, William, 166, 167, 168, 169

South, Donald, illus. #20

Sowers, Forrest, 44

Spinola, Abbie, 45

Stafford, George, 8, 9-10, 111; illus. #20

Stafford, Helen. *See* Vandegrift, Helen Stafford

Stafford, Ida. *See* Fenstermacher, Ida Stafford

Stafford, Kathryn McDowell, **9-10**; illus. #7

Stafford, Sarah. *See* Walker, Sarah Stafford

Sterner, Sister Gunnell, 153, **162-164**

Strowig, Ernestine. *See* Pilant, Ernestine Strowig

Strowig, Fred, 8, **12**, 13, 14, 24, 111; illus. #13, #23

Sulak, Al, 12

Swope, Bobby, 133

T

Tabor Children's Services, ii, v, 173

Tabor Home for Children

farm work and, 2-3, 18, 21, 27, 29, 33, 36, 50, 80, 88-89, 103, 105

history of, iii-iv

home canning and, 13, 54, 58, 61, 98, 105

life during the Depression, 7, 12, 20, 24, 25, 27

life during World War II, 61, 89, 119

physical description of, 4, 58-60, 82-84

schooling and, 7, 9, 12, 18, 20, 24, 26, 64-65, 71, 84, 85, 87-88, 100, 109, 126-127, 129, 132, 140-141, 169

sports and, 12, 18, 20, 36, 42-45, 47, 49, 63, 64, 85, 86, 92, 105, 127, 157

Tacker, Marian, 126, 138

Tenley, Bruce, 79

Thomas, Russ, 42

Tindall, Jane Fritz, 75, 104, 106, **107-108**

Trettin, Walter, 18, 111

Trout, Frank, 49

V

Vandegrift, Helen Stafford, 8, 111

Vrancken, Wynona, 171

W

Walker, Sarah Stafford, 8, 111; illus. #20

Waller, Charles, **170-172**

Walton, Sandy, 97-98

Watson, Cathy Welch, 126, **132-134**, 138, 145; illus. #23

Welch, Cathy. *See* Watson, Cathy Welch

Welch, Johnny, 132

Welch, Kay. *See* Watson, Cathy Welch

Welch, Peggy, 132; illus. #23

Wenzloff, Arnold, **95-96**; illus. #10

West, Diane, 171

Whiteside, Ann Osgood, **135-137**; illus. #23

Willow Grove Naval Base, 159

Wilson, Jean, 138, 147

Wilson, Mary. *See* Schaffer, Mary Wilson

Winkle, Ted, 18

Wohlfarth, Herb, 12

Wolfe, Bill, 12, 49

Wood, Mary Ralston, 124

Wright, Orville, i, 49, 52, **82-94**, 99, 115, 144, 173; illus. #10, #23

visits Joe Hoppe, **75-81**

writes to Sister Wilma, 124-125

Wright, Wilbur, 52, 83, 85, 86, 89, 90, 94, 99, 105, 115; illus. #10

writes to Sister Wilma, 124

Wrigley, William (Justice of the Peace), 99, 119

Y

Yost, Margaret Schmaltz, illus. #23

Youells, Joan Bach, **138-139**; illus. #2